COPPERNICK

number 27 / fall 2018

D1036410

EDITOR/MANAGING EDITOR
Wayne Miller

EDITORS: POETRY
Brian Barker
Nicky Beer

EDITOR: FICTION & NONFICTION
Joanna Luloff

EDITOR: FICTION
Teague Bohlen

CONSULTING EDITORS: FICTION
Alexander Lumans
Christopher Merkner

SENIOR EDITORS
Karl Chwe
Darryl Ellison
Sammi Johnson
Taylor Kirby
Elise Lakey
Vin Nagle
Lyn Poats
Kyra Scrimgeour

ASSOCIATE EDITORS
Larysa Labiak
Chiahci Lee
Amanda Pruess
Amber Sullivan
Tristian Thanh
Grace Wagner

ASSISTANT EDITORS
Alli Ackerman
Padideh Aghanoury
Win Doak
Portia Graf
Kayla Gropp
Jessie Hawk
Ven Hickenbottom
Madeline Johnson
Kara Klein
Isaac Leigh
Holly McCloskey

Emily Mullis
Amy Scott
Ali Sensintaffar
Nathan Smith
Karley Sun
Hannah Thomas
LeShaye Williams
Alec Witthohn

INTERNS
Steph Rowden
Steven Vigil-Roach

CONTRIBUTING EDITORS
Robert Archambeau
Mark Brazaitis
Geoffrey Brock
A. Papatya Bucak
Victoria Chang
Martha Collins
Robin Ekiss
Tarfia Faizullah
V. V. Ganeshananthan
Kevin Haworth
Joy Katz
David Keplinger
Jesse Lee Kercheval
Jason Koo
Thomas Legendre
Randall Mann
Adrian Matejka
Pedro Ponce
Kevin Prufer
Frederick Reiken
James Richardson
Emily Ruskovich
Eliot Khalil Wilson

ART CONSULTANTS
Maria Elena Buszek
Adam Lerner

OFFICE MANAGERS
Maria Alvarez
Francine Olivas-Zarate

COPPERNICKEL

Copper Nickel is the national literary journal housed at the University of Colorado Denver. Published in March and October, it features poetry, fiction, essays, and translation folios by established and emerging writers. We welcome submissions from all writers and currently pay $30 per printed page. Submissions are assumed to be original and unpublished. For more information, please visit **copper-nickel.org**. Subscriptions are available—and at discounted rates for students—at regonline. com/coppernickelsubscriptions. *Copper Nickel* is distributed nationally through Publishers Group West (PGW) and Media Solutions, and digitally catalogued by EBSCO. We are deeply grateful for the support of the Department of English and the College of Liberal Arts & Sciences at the University of Colorado Denver, as well as to Culture Ireland for their support of this issue's Irish/UK Poets Feature.

Culture Ireland
Cultúr Éireann

Contents

FEATURE
Fourteen Poets from Ireland and the United Kingdom

Conor O'Callaghan
61 / In Memory of the Recent Past
64 / Upon the Very Nature of Loss

Lorna Shaughnessy
65 / Bishop's Quay

Paul Perry
66 / Leonora's Violin

Vahni Capildeo
67 / Everything Becomes Holy at Six O'Clock

James Byrne
68 / The Triumph of Fire

Chrissy Williams
69 / Casual Arousal in Murnau's *Faust*
70 / *Extract from* Recovered Text Drafts

Elaine Feeney
71 / Buy yourself a routine. Run like clockwerk. Take the pills.

Sam Riviere
74 / Regime of Signs
75 / In the Provinces

Zoë Brigley
76 / Un/dressing Beatitudes

Martin Dyar
79 / Flannery

Jessica Traynor
81 / Photographing the Dead

Stephen Sexton
83 / O,

Victoria Kennefick
85 / Corpus Christi Procession

Manuela Moser
87 / On writing about my grandfather

FICTION

Farah Ali
3 / Present Tense

Amy Stuber
42 / People's Parties

Jacinda Townsend
89 / Veneer

Jyotsna Sreenivasan
129 / The Crystal Vase: Snapshots

NONFICTION

Kathryn Nuernberger
27 / The Long Lost Friend

Stuart Friebert
101 / Sorry, I Don't

Ira Sukrungruang
158 / When We Are Done Vanishing

POETRY

Emily J. Cousins
1 / Poem at the Entrance

L. S. Klatt
2 / Declaration

Francis Santana
13 / A Tiger
14 / Nourishment
15 / Unpromised Land

Caitlin Roach
17 / to bernadette

Corey Marks
18 / Conversation with a Dead Cicada

Paul Otremba
22 / Cabin in the Woods
24 / Hail the Lizard

Becka Mara McKay
26 / [DONKEY'S BREAKFAST: A straw
mattress in a sailor's bunk]

Jonathan Weinert
48 / The Story of My Life

Michael Pontacoloni
51 / Neutral Buoyancy Laboratory

Emily Skaja
52 / Dear Emily

Kathleen McGookey
54 / The School of Anguish
55 / The Haunting

Christopher Kempf
56 / Senior Night

Christopher Warner
58 / Enhanced Interrogation Techniques

Erika Jo Brown
107 / Mary Ruefle Poem

Juan Morales
108 / Secret Maintenance

Molly Spencer
109 / Disclosures | If You Are Aware of Any Nuisance
Animals Such as Crows, Chickens, or Barking Dogs

Arthur Russell
111 / Burning Garbage

Vanessa Stauffer
115 / Jean de Fiennes (The Young Man)

Mike White
138 / Inn

Michael Homolka
140 / On the Disappointing Nature of Spirituality

T. R. Hummer
141 / Spat
142 / A Monument

Hera Naguib
143 / Self-Portrait as a Khamba in a Sabzi Mandi in Lahore

Paige Quiñones
144 / Still Life with Wadded Paper Towels

Jessica Lynn Suchon
145 / Ars Poetica with Post Traumatic Stress Disorder

Chelsea Wagenaar
163 / September Psalm

Jenny Boychuk
164 / Doctor's Appointment, After Her Death
166 / Half-Moon Elegy

Corey Van Landingham
168 / Great American Ball Park

John Koethe
170 / Tempting Fate

Benjamin S. Grossberg
172 / Missed Connections

TRANSLATION FOLIOS

Carsten René Nielsen
33 / Five Poems, introduced & translated by David Keplinger

Khal Torabully
119 / Four Poems, introduced & translated by Nancy Naomi Carlson

Cristina Rivera Garza
147 / Three Poems, introduced & translated by Julia Leverone

Bios / 175

Required Reading / 183

On the Cover / Kristen Hatgi Sink, *Milk & Honey*
Pigment print on 100% rag paper with UV coating, 35" x 52", 2015

(for more on Hatgi Sink's work, visit www.kristenhatgi.com)

EMILY J. COUSINS

Poem at the Entrance

I can hear the front move in
pushed from the canyon mouth
I can hear the jet cut the sky
crosscurrent I hear my pulse
ripple out empty pause
here come the big feelings

L. S. KLATT

Declaration

I wrote I love you on litmus & dropped
it in the grass where it was picked up by
Thomas Jefferson, who would sleep along

the fence & crawl into the light to sun
himself. Years later, when I returned
wearing a paper suit, I saw his body

being questioned. Soon after, I said
to the litmus, you are not the valentine
I supposed but a false positive.

The authorities gave my tongue a local
anesthetic. It blunted the pain
& made it possible for me to speak

my piece, as I did, quoting the Virginian.
I've changed my story several times since,
albeit the ichor is real, the wound literal.

FARAH ALI

Present Tense

WHAT I REMEMBER MOST FROM childhood is a time when my father did not come home one day, and not the next day, nor the day after. I was twelve then and my brother was fifteen. In the first few days of his absence, I used to wake up in a state of anxiety, my body filling up with the unpleasantness of this great uncertainty my brother, my mother and I were thrust into. I felt better among the wooden, lidded desks in my classroom and the faces of my teachers, and by afternoon recess I was at the peak of my day's happiness. In the evening, as six o'clock came nearer, the time my father usually came home, I was paralyzed with worry and could only sit in a corner of the living room, only able to move again when the hour hand came to rest on seven. After a strange meal with my shrunken family I used to sink into sleep, grateful that my father was still gone, and uncomfortable with myself for feeling this way.

I wanted to be assured of his staying away longer but didn't know how to talk to my mother about him. Besides, my brother was already doing the asking. She gave him a different answer each time. "He is visiting relatives." Or, "He needs to be at work." Or, "He comes home late and goes to work before you wake up." One evening she was humming and sorting out a pile of old books and maybe that made my brother wonder if she had killed our father. His face turned red and he shouted at her and called her selfish. She paused in her task and said, sharp as ice, "Your father is perfectly fine." She always called him "your father" when she was angry and wanted to hold us, his sons, responsible for his presence as if our births made him a necessary evil in her life. And when she said those two words that night I felt twisted with sadness because I'd thought that with him gone she would like her sons better. My brother stomped away but I stood a while longer, watching her face anxiously. I felt light only when she started to hum again.

•

MY FATHER HAS come to the airport to pick me up. I feel jittery and uncertain, reduced from my adult height to a child's dimensions. But I keep control of my suitcase and make sure he sees me tipping a porter even though we haven't taken his help, and by the time we have walked to the car I am a grownup again. I have not been in Karachi for seven years; I have not sat next to my father for just as long. He is old now, and his fingers curved over the steering wheel are thin. He peers through the windshield and drives in bursts of speed, dodging motorcycles and rickshaws. His window is rolled down and he instructs me to do the same.

"Cross ventilation," he says over the noise of a bus horn.

I say, "We should get the air conditioner fixed."

"There's no need to throw away good money," he says. "You don't understand."

I pull out my cell phone even though there isn't anyone I need to assure that I have arrived safely.

"Put that away," my father says. "Put it under you. Don't you read the news?"

I wonder why I have chosen to be here again. A lump grows in my stomach the closer we get to the house I grew up in. I struggle to stay in the future, thinking about the day I will return to the airport and fly across comforting barriers of mountains and oceans to my other continent, to my other city where problems come in neat packages no bigger than the palm of my hand. When that fails I try to ground myself in the very seconds of the present—the feel of the thin car seat cover, the roughness of my nails. And sometimes a new underpass or a flyover or a shiny new mall distracts me and that is good, until I see a piece of wall I often passed when I was little, and I am again pulled thinly, painfully, through that narrow corridor between the past and the future; between that which we can never change and that which gives us a chance to escape.

•

MY BROTHER BLAMED our mother. He watched her through narrowed eyes.

"She knows where he is. She is lying to us," he said to me at least twice a day.

If we were in the school van and I was laughing at something a friend had said, he would pinch me and hiss those words into my ear. I would immediately turn away from the joke and remove the grin from my face.

"Do you miss him? Our father?" he would ask me in a tight voice.

I would lie and say, "Yes. Of course I do."

WE had grown up on thin air in the house, the oxygen sucked up by our father and mother's moods. We were curved and wiry and tense like antennae, picking up signals of impending storms from the way our father snapped his newspaper or how our mother shut the fridge door. Too sharp a sound meant that soon old wounds were going to be reopened with blade-like words. Sometimes I mouthed along those words, being my father and mother by turns like an actor playing two roles. Other times I went to my brother and found him elaborately coloring in a map, or a picture of the human heart, or an eyeball, or the circulation system.

He wanted me to have a good opinion of our father. He said that a long time ago, before we were born, our father had gone without a lot of things so he could save money for his future children. He had eaten only one solid meal a day, did not have chicken except once a month, and walked to most places under the blazing sun. Then when he had enough money, he got this whole house built just for us. He put three bedrooms in it, each a different color—yellow, green, and blue. The boundary wall surrounding the house was also an example of how much he cared—it had shards of glass set on the top to stop burglars from climbing over and robbing him of his possessions.

From the other room, we heard a roar.

My brother said, "You can see why he's like that, right? It's because of *her*. He can't help it."

•

MY MOTHER HAS given me the firmest mattress in the house and put a brand-new bed-sheet over it. There is no comforter, only a second sheet. It is too warm for anything thicker. I am in my old room, of course. In some places the yellow paint has started flaking off the wall in irregular shapes and I have the urge to peel them. I count three brown arches of water stains in corners. The bathroom mirror is speckled and my face appears gray.

"Do you need more money?" I ask my mother. I am unable to meet her eyes, guilty that I have not been here earlier, that I already want to leave.

"We are comfortable, son," she says.

She makes me two *rotis* and watches me eat. She complains about my brother. I ask her to give him a call and she says, "He is happy in his own life. He has no regard for us."

I speak to him that night. He lives in another continent, a third one. He has not visited Karachi in close to ten years. I tell him the house looks small and helpless, and that things aren't what they used to be; they are peaceful. He tells me he is done talking and hands the phone to his wife. I tell her my brother ought to come see his old parents, and she explains to me that his doctor—his therapist—says that he is prone to melancholia and being back there will make him morose which is bad for their children, who are precious and innocent.

My brother still thinks that our father—and maybe our mother—owe us an explanation and an apology.

•

WHENEVER THEY FOUGHT it was my mother who looked crazy. Her hair came out of her bun, her breath expelled itself loudly through her nostrils and teeth, her fists bunched up. She also had a way of moaning and clutching her clothes. Once I watched, terrified and fascinated, as she picked up a slipper and slapped her own thighs. She liked to grab my arm and say to my father, in a tearful, triumphant way, "I have my children. I have *my* children." That always made me feel happy and strong, and I glowered at my father. I promised to myself that if he offered to drive me to school I would say no.

When he wasn't roaring, he was unremarkable in his shape and size. He was thin and walked with a slight slouch which made him appear genial. His eyes when amused were mild. He liked to tell me and my brother that we had a lot to learn, and took us with him on errands. He spoke kindly to petrol station attendants and mechanics, and if their skin was the same dark brown as his he gave them a tip and told them a joke.

"These are our brothers, hard-working immigrants from India," he would say to us. "Look how they sweat for their bread."

He spoke as if he were correcting a fault in us.

We would pass a plot of land where light-skinned men burned red from the sun would be carrying bricks, disappearing behind new walls of other people's houses. Sometimes one of them would look up and his eyes would flash green or blue.

Our father would point to the men and say, "Watch out for these lazy, dirty people, come down from the north to cause us trouble, setting up shacks. You know that bomb that went off in Lyari? Them. That riot in Saddar? Them."

I worried that these men looked like my mother even though her eyes were brown.

Once I asked her where she was from and she laughed and said, "Here. I was born right here in Karachi."

•

MY BROTHER TELLS me that he wants to come see our parents. His voice is very robust on the phone, and he says his therapist thinks he is ready to take this step. He says he will start looking into his schedule and flights. He might even bring the wife and children.

His heartiness is like an ill-fitting coat.

I take my father to an eye doctor, to get him a pair of glasses. He goes through the tests with grim resignation.

Back in the car he says, "That was an Urdu-speaking doctor, which is why I let him check me."

A little later he points to a string of shops. "New businesses going up everywhere. Karachi is still the City of Lights." And he looks at me as if I have challenged him.

•

FOR MANY EVENINGS my brother waited by the window for our father, sitting on a chair with his knees drawn up to his chin. He stopped playing with his friends. One day on our way home from school we saw a bus on fire. As the driver pressed hard on the brake and turned around the school van, my friends and I leaned out and saw flames leaping out of the bus's windows like so many strange passengers. There were some men around it, yelling and laughing. One of them drew back his arm and, with the grace of a javelin thrower at the Olympics, hurled his lit-up torch at the bus. The driver shouted at us to get away from the windows and to shut them. The men might attack us next. My brother drew his head in reluctantly.

He started buying newspapers from the shop at the corner and looked through them all, reading out loud reports of kidnappings of activists, of their bodies found in trash heaps.

"Our father is one of them. He's been taken away," he said.

I imagined our father in the back of a black car with tinted windows, a man with a long mustache next to him with a rifle on his lap. My brother told me to help him read the papers; if I said I was bored, he pounded the floor with his fist and said I was turning into our mother. So I bent my head again, peeling skin off my heels and toes, while names rolled by in front of my eyes, a monotonous landscape sketched in black ink.

He made me search the house at night after our mother was asleep. He said he was looking for clues that might point to our father. Once, he wanted to check if our mother was one of the enemy agents so we went into the kitchen and twisted open jars of spices and sniffed the contents for suspicious substances. We discovered that entering our parents' room was as easy as pushing their door open. We went there only one time, though. Our mother was all by herself, frowning in her sleep. My brother motioned for me to look under her bed, and I wondered what he would say if I found a gun there. But there was nothing except a pair of our father's slippers. I gave them to my brother and he held them to his chest.

Some nights he soundlessly turned the key in the front door and we went out to the lawn. The grass felt soothing under the tender, raw bottoms of my feet. I would stand with my brother in the dark until the sky began to lighten. Then we would go in to change for school.

ONE afternoon he forbade me from playing with our classmates and made me stand next to him right outside our gate.

"We have to meet someone," he said.

I thought he had made a new friend, and I felt sorry for him when the sun began to go down and still no one came. I watched other fathers arrive home, their cars pulling tiredly through the gates of their houses. I imagined the men climbing out slowly in crumpled shirts and pants, collars unstarched from the day's work, smelling of cigarettes and exhaust fumes, like ours used to. I wondered what my father was doing, but I wondered about him as I would about people in an airplane passing overhead. We turned around and went back home, walking by our father's dusty car in the garage. On the weekend my brother washed it and made it shine. He said it made our father feel closer to him.

•

MY BROTHER HAS curled himself up on his bed and not gone to work for three days now, his wife tells me. She has sent their two children to her mother's until he feels better, and she has asked his therapist to come over. My sister-in-law is a competent woman, not given to hysteria. She has probably washed a set of dishes and run the washing machine while speaking to the doctor. I ask her if I ought to come and she says that will not do anyone any good.

THERE has been no electricity in the house all morning. My father is reading a newspaper, taking off his glasses every few minutes to rub the bridge of his nose. My mother is asleep on the sofa, her face shiny. I think about making a list of things that they both need. Hand rails in the bathrooms? A generator, a driver, a full-time maid? A new house, a different continent? Not mine or my brother's but another of their very own, so that we all might have space and live in happiness?

I doze off and wake up a while later to the sound of my father's voice. My stomach contracts, but he is only telling my mother to go sit by the open window because there is a good breeze coming through; he says he will sleep somewhere else.

•

WHILE MY FATHER was gone, my mother turned very beautiful. She grew her thinnest and her skin became so pale it was almost transparent. When she stood under a strong light I could see little blue veins on her face. She started to wear perfume and she held our books daintily so as not to ruin her polished fingernails. After my brother poured her bottle of nail color down the sink she kept her nails bare again. One evening he slapped down a newspaper in front of her and told her to check it for our father's name among victims of recent incidents. She ran her fingertip down the lists and articles detailing riots and mobs, but I felt she wasn't really reading; she was thinking about getting her hair done at the salon.

Two months went by, and if she thought about our father or missed him she didn't say so. She didn't mention him at all. In the morning, she waited with us for the school van and told us that we were not to step outside until the last bell rang and that we were to come straight home. She shook her head and wished we didn't have to go so far away, trouble could start anywhere in the city at any time. She moved toward my brother but he stepped away from her reach, so she busied herself with straightening my tie. She put her hands on my shoulders and said, "People are disappearing."

I was buoyed by her concern and did well in all my tests. In the mirror, I practiced smiles of gratitude that I could give her. When she sat at the table with us now she leaned forward, her back a letter C, and this new pliancy made me unable to speak sometimes.

Before my father left, she would often come out of the kitchen with a big knife in her hand and slam it on the table. Then she would flip through our schoolwork and if one of us had gotten a sum wrong or had done untidy writing she would throw the book at the wall or run a sharpened pencil down the page. Under the table, I would pick the skin around my nails into tiny pieces, eyeing the blade, because I was sure that one day my mother would run it through us. All of us.

My mother's friend came to visit her one evening. She brushed our hair off our foreheads and clicked her tongue and looked at us as if we had suddenly become fatherless boys, irreversibly so. She told us to take her little girl out to the lawn while the grownups talked. We sat on the grass and pulled up a few blades.

The girl asked, "Where is your father?"

My brother frowned and said, "He has gone for work."

"I heard our cleaning woman say he's left his wife and his children," she said.

My brother lunged toward her and grabbed her hair in his fist and said, "Shut up."

•

I WANT TO TAKE my parents out to eat.

Truthfully, I do not want to take them anywhere, but that is what a good son does—fix his parents' health, improve their home, spoil them, because one spent her body in giving birth and the other worked at a job he did not like; because they stayed together for their children's sake; because they endured enormous pain believing they were doing us good.

MY mother says she wants to have Chinese food. My father wants to know why I like to waste my money. In the car, he puts a small cushion behind my mother's back and asks her how much she wants her window rolled down. They are extremely cheerful on the way to the restaurant. They point out all the work being done in the city.

"Look at that excavator," my father says.

"I don't see any piles of garbage here anymore," my mother says. "Tell me if you see any garbage."

"You should come back and settle down here, son," my father says. "Get married."

The present is slipping away from me again, and I rub my fingers hard over the worn rubber on the steering wheel. Five thin scratches on the windshield, black dashboard, truck in side mirror.

Our father used to take us out sometimes on Thursdays, the last day of the work week. My mother brushed our hair until it lay flat across our heads, and we wore shirts with collars and full pants. She got dressed in soft colors and let her plait hang down her back instead of keeping it coiled viciously in a bun. In the car and during the meal she and my father parried gently-teasing words in low murmurs, his voice smooth and sure and content, hers full of secrets her children couldn't guess. I did not know how to participate in this sort of behavior, this display of affection. Maybe I had imagined seeing them spit at each other. I felt unsettled and even a little happy, the way an unpopular, blindfolded child in a game feels.

•

AROUND NINE ONE night, after our mother had gone to sleep, my brother sat on the edge of my bed and said that we had something important to do. He had shadows under his eyes, I remember, and his face looked small and square. I followed him through doors and over the grass and when he started undoing the bolts of the gate I felt a spasm of fear in case our father had been hiding outside every night and was going to leap back in now, full of anger that we had kept him locked out. But there was nobody there, not even a beggar. There was a curfew in the city and everything had shut at eight. I wanted to whisper, "Where are we going?" but my brother was now taking long strides and the words stayed inside me and I went with him. We reached the end of the street and I saw someone squatting on the dirt, next to the trunk of an acacia tree. The figure stood up when we stopped and I could only tell that it was a man. I still remember how he smelled—of roses.

My brother held out an envelope. "Where is my father?" he said.

"Hand over the money first," the man said, muffled behind his scarf.

"First the information, son of a pig."

I remember my brother's voice, steadied by rage. I remember the man's white hand, the color my father preferred not to shake, grabbing the envelope and my brother trying to twist it out of his grasp. I remember his small gray silhouette dwarfed by the man's large one. I remember the man sinking a blade into my brother's leg and then running away. My brother crumpled onto the gravel and I think I was worried that he couldn't be comfortable there.

I do not remember the walk back home, or waking up my mother.

She said we needed to take my brother to a hospital. I sat next to him, holding a shirt over the wound on his thigh, the blood spreading up, away from gravity, onto my fingers. My mother started the engine and I had a sudden memory of me and my brother, very small and still, watching from that same place in the back as our mother sat in the driver's seat, pale and pinched as a starved moon, gripping the steering wheel with bloodless hands, listening to our father tell her she was too dumb to learn. We watched him grab the wheel and weave the car wildly to the left and right. I don't think she had ever tried to drive again. But that night she drove, grimly and slowly. On a side street, she stopped in front of a small house with a crescent and a star painted on its wall. Inside the poorly lit examination room there was a doctor and he checked my brother's injured leg. The sound of my brother's moans seemed to have brought out small children from other parts of the doctor's house and they ran around the room barefoot, shrieking with happiness.

It took a couple of weeks for my brother's injury to heal, and another month for the three of us to not think about that night every night, when one day we came home from school and saw our father sitting on the sofa, wearing formal clothes as if he had just come home early from work on a whim. He got up when he saw us and tried to pat our backs but couldn't because we had our school bags on so he let his arm fall to the side. There was no mark on his face, no fracture in his leg. He looked unbroken and clean shaven. There was a small suitcase by his feet, the kind that people take with them when they deliberately choose to leave, filling it with things they want to take. "I'll leave the black socks and keep the brown ones," he might have said. "I'll leave the children and keep the distance." Perhaps my mother had helped him pack.

It seemed to me that he had said something. "Have you been good children?" he might have asked us.

He pulled out a leather jacket from the suitcase and told my brother that it was for him. I remember the smell of it—sharp and old. My brother put it on and then stood there self-consciously, the jacket hanging over his skinny frame, his Adam's apple bobbing up and down nervously, his face flushed. My father gave me a shirt wrapped in cellophane. It was blue and had a collar. I took it and didn't say anything. Next to me I could feel my brother shaking, and I wondered, as if from far away, if he also understood that our father had never really become one of the missing ones of the city, those written about in newspapers and lauded for martyrdom. Our mother brought out cups of tea for all of us, and our father turned on the news.

•

"Are you having a good time there? Is mother spoiling you? Does she remember she has two sons?" asks my brother.

I think, *That is the work of his medication.* I have learned by now to say the right things when he is at this stage of his recovery.

"I'd forgotten how hot summer can be here," I say, raising my eyebrows and gesturing with my free hand as if I am on a stage and my brother is in the audience.

There is a pause, maybe a minute long, maybe two.

"I can't go there just yet," he says. "I looked, you know, and there's just no time, no time at all. The children's school, all this work. You should have planned this better. I would have come along. Maybe June. Would you be there in June? Would you stay there for me?"

That evening I sit with a large calendar on my lap and a marker in my hand. My mother is next to me, her finger on December.

She says, very loudly, "What do you think about winter? We could get the house repainted, put beds for his children?" She is indirectly addressing my father but not looking at him, so she can keep herself intact if he ignores her.

He has heard her, I know, but does not respond. Old, familiar nervousness fills my stomach, when my mother turns to me and says, "Maybe April next year. Spring holidays for your brother's family, and you. That would give me time to prepare. For the furniture."

I draw a circle for her in the April square and she hangs it back on the wall. It is the wrong year, but that does not matter.

FRANCIS SANTANA

A Tiger

I want to conceive a tiger,
repetitive, grave,
bound to contradictions.
It will bear the faces
of people who never loved me.
It will roar like a deity
in the catacombs, abandoned,
hungry, disillusioned.
It will develop slowly,
out of old memories,
out of photographs I keep
for retribution. I will write to my father
lying about the patterns
etched on its hide.
I will raise it away
from Neruda & Whitman,
feed it geometry & numbers.
It will devour whoever approaches it
with tenderness.
It will prowl violently
in my slumber,
stalking the people
who have found ways
to live without me.
It will grow as big as a constellation,
and one day when its claws reach
for what is left of you,
I will pull out a sharp knife, the one stuck
between desolation & my ribcage,
slash its throat, swiftly:
No one will mind a poet
leading deliverance through slaughter.

Nourishment

I starve my body until it learns
how to survive on small victories.

Like when the wind dies
in the Atlantic, unnamed,
without fuss or

when a stray dog presumes
a branch is the hand of God

so he sits under its shadows,
barks at men who are forced
to trek in the heat, instead

of shaming them
into sharing what they carry home.

Today I fed myself a feast
to celebrate a black boy

who had called his mother
to announce his path
back across the city. But

by the time the last crumb
had measured the length
between my hand and my throat

they had found his body, resting

under a sycamore devoured
by bronze beetles.

I still waste in his rubble.

Unpromised Land

There are no honeybees in this poem
hurried in their hand-me-down uniforms
pulling on each other's long sleeves before diving

into Cosmos, sometimes proverbial,
sometimes brimming enough pollen to feed
the errand wasp that loots without apology.

I see them from my window, thirsting
across the valley that lets itself be gobbled up
by darkness and meager metaphors.

But there's a crowd of mothers
pushed against a galvanized fence,
the chain link meant to outlast the cheek.

You will hear a laptop, a television
drumming to the beat of a boy's short strokes,
the diligence of fist-size ammunition.

Maybe this is where I'm supposed to spot
a simile about how wounds and
split watermelons melt among the rubble.

Maybe this is where I list the things
they carry, the things abandoned,
the things misplaced along the way.

65 million people have no home,
& they wander, & they hunger, & they cry
like 65 million people who have no home.

I'm sure there's a jacaranda there
that grows from the seeds in someone's pocket.
Maybe, if you look hard enough

you'll sing to all the carved names.
I want to believe that among them
a group of friends gathers around a radio,

the way you gather around a fire
to call upon the spirits, & they blab-along
the Wu-Tang Clan, & they hum to each other
about the milk they might never drink.

CAITLIN ROACH

to bernadette

—after *The End of the Alphabet*

barn swallow / waxwing / auklet
     crested / sweetmilk / it will nudge all soft
     of the shell from within.

     sacrum / coccyx / the color of some irruptive season
         ripening on the tongue / the taste of blood on it
         the backs and betweens of some little mouth
         (open, meaning empty)

         —those who yielded to your slow grace, darkened, as by shadow

as the cocoon, gutted
     unfledged thews draining from the cleft

     —feels damaged enough to give and still
     the body charms, hurled against the wall.

     when they found the body, there had been something living in it.
         something growing in it.

COREY MARKS

Conversation with a Dead Cicada

The racket's gone out of you,
or the song, rather—no more flogging yourself
into your own restless GPS.

How like yourself you look, though,
on the heat-stressed asphalt,
your glassy wings crazed

with orange and black,
folded back, intact
as a specimen's in a museum.

Magicicada tredecim a little tag would read
if I leaned toward the glass to see
an example as pristine as you,

one among rows arranged
like a neighborhood
seen from a satellite,

though a smudge from some kid's nose
would distort the view, a cloud
bearing in some disaster lingering

long after the kid has run ahead,
impatient to see it all, or bored
with everything he finds.

It's possible to pay too little attention
and still want more than everything
the world already yields.

Or perhaps he just wanted to be home,
and left alone, left to his own devices.
Like you those thirteen years

beneath someone's lawn. Your time
was different than mine—
you didn't attend that other world:

footsteps and shadows, the indignities
of the neighbors' dogs, election signs
hammered into place, wrenched out,

the rains, the marvels and discontents,
the periodic whine of a mower
a distant song. What difference to you—

numb, blind, deaf, lodged
in stubborn soil
with one long change to occupy you

until a voice rent you through,
an incessant claim.
And now, little singer,

little all-sung-out, we have
this corner. There used to be
a school in that field.

Children's voices trailed me,
mornings, on my walk.
Once, a girl perched

in the branches of the oak—
silent, staring down. A dour bird.
A hieroglyph I couldn't translate.

I looked away, ashamed
for intruding. And there,
a man I haven't seen for years

stood on his stoop and called
as I passed, "Get a real job."
Perhaps he was right.

America fumbled at two wars then,
and gnashed at itself like an animal
irritated by its skin. And I had

my own changes to occupy me.
My daughter was born. My father died.
I lost a lovely dog.

But when your brood first clambered
from the soil into all that yattering,
you were news. And then,

well, I've felt it, too, the world
losing interest, turning less
and less politely away.

Even now a cloud smudges our sky,
a god of boredom, of the next
exhaustible thrill. I can't help but think

it's that kid from the museum again,
streaking his face across the glass,
looking and looking his fill.

He's taken with my silly smile
tilted over you cattywampus
in my palm, taken with the randomness

of our being on a street
in a neighborhood
that could well be his, but isn't.

The cloud scoots closer.
The sun blears out. The light
glazes over. Then how quickly

he tires of us, another whim
he's flitting past—
already he's beyond

the dormant houses
with their rooflines pitched,
wings folded back,

refusing, like you, their songs.

PAUL OTREMBA

Cabin in the Woods

We are at the point when the attic's antique lock
already is hacked open, when the trapdoor's dropped
on the preacher's hidden playroom, and clothes fall
across the seats of the borrowed convertible,
while the city is faraway but still awake

beneath the overlook, where no one's looking out
for what they should be, and the burial sleep
has been kicked up carelessly, because the dare
held the promise of touching, because a hint
of buttons strained to be undone, because it was raining

and there was nowhere to go besides this house—
empty—kept like a secret by kudzu off the road,
because the wealth of other lives is such a steal
at yard sales, who could say no to the music box,
the carved mask, the ancient and yellowing diary

with its small Latin script, a living hand—grasping
and capable—caught below the surface? For this night
(which is night because how else is this happening)
you get to feel chosen. Like splintered pallets of wood
whose destinies are always to impale skulkers

of dark alleys, like the stripped bones and torn T-shirts
that mean torches for the dungeon's safe passage.
You even get a choice, your own devil shuffling cards
at the crossroads: this way, the table saw; here, the exit
wound; or Tunnel #3 for the breadcrumb-trail of blood

toward the final girl. There's no plot hole good violence
can't satisfy. In *these* worlds, with confidence, pull off
to change your tire after midnight inside the forest.
Pull in to this southern town where the motel is pure
vacancy. Trespass here is a foregone conclusion; prejudice,

incidental. So pound the stranger's door in your need.
The gauze of clouds across the moon will dim
your location among the houses. The stalks in the field
touch suddenly in chorus like so many wings. The emergency
axe hangs in the hallway waiting for someone's good idea.

Hail the Lizard

The green anole lizard might
                    turn this way off
            its perch on the foxtail fern

into the circle of resting cats
                    or this way cutting a clear path
            to the cat's-claw vines invading

every seam in the fence.
                    At some point you just admit
            you're what remains of the tick

pinched free from the dog's flank
                    for constantly bringing to attention
            that the poet meant

perspective not resolve,
                    as in the anole's choice
            between two dark routes lying

equally in barb-cloaking leaves.
                    The poetry of the anole is not
            pedagogy. You are the sum total

of the anole leaping through
                    the lion's den of only half-sleepers
            who chase it up the fig tree.

You are the flash of the anole
                    toward the millipede, lost traveller
            on the concrete slab, and you are

the rival locked in the anole's jaw,
                    your triumph warming under
            a full sun. You are the dewlap's red

sun of warning, pulsing
              from the trees. To fall down
       the face of the world, so effortlessly,

to venture out onto the thinnest
              tongue of leaf, to be the hunger
       that hides in plain sight, false

chameleon, to be the anole
              out of the cats' reach and the one
       whipping in the blue jay's beak.

BECKA MARA McKAY

[DONKEY'S BREAKFAST:
A straw mattress in a sailor's bunk]

We slept on straw when straw was safer
than the ground, believing the body's final

home has power. We slept on the ground
when the ground was safer than the trees,

believing in bone and ash and the last place
the body makes itself comfortable.

We slept in the trees to escape the jaws
of our enemies, honoring the last place

the body faced its fears. We slept in the jaws
of our enemies to understand hunger.

We mark the last place the body removes
its shoes, or holds another body,

or pays attention to the other bodies
all around. We slept in hunger when we

sought God. We remember the last place
the body gives up, the last place the body

rests: tree or tomb or miles below the sea's green
knuckles. When we were finished we slept in God.

KATHRYN NUERNBERGER

The Long Lost Friend

A WELL-LAID HEX CAN LAST a long time. *Pow-Wow, or Long Lost Friend: A Collection of Mysterious and Invaluable Arts and Remedies for Man as well as Animals, with Many Proofs of Their Virtue and Efficacy in Healing Diseases, Etc.*, was an Americanized English translation of a very old book of spells and home remedies. From the German tradition of braucherai, it was translated as "pow-wow," in keeping with the many other appropriations that would be committed by the European immigrants against Algonquin and other indigenous peoples.

Long Lost Friend has spells, charms, and recipes. Any and all of these were called a hex or a pow-wow. In this book, the line between magic and folk wisdom is not a line. To prevent a wicked or malicious person from doing you an injury, you should recite the following: "Dullix, ix, ux. Yea you can't come over Pontio, Pontio is above Pilato." To cure epilepsy, take a turtle dove, cut its throat, and let the person afflicted with epilepsy drink the blood. For the spell "To Prevent Gun-Barrels from Rusting," you will need an ounce of bear's fat, half an ounce of badger's grease, half an ounce of snake's fat, one ounce of almond oil, and a quarter of an ounce of pulverized indigo. There are spells to make molasses and beer, recipes for eye-water, words to protect a traveler on a journey, remedies for burns and colic in this book.

To hear John Blymire tell it, the hex Nelson Rehmeyer put on him had lasted his whole life, from the moment he was born.

To hear Nelson Rehmeyer tell it, Who is John Blymire and why would I curse a man I don't know, or anybody at all?

We used to live not so very far from the place where John Blymire murdered Nelson Rehmeyer. A state away, but still inside the orbit of all those old hex signs on the barns and whispers of this or that granny woman and what folks remember of how she used to heal, our defunct dairy farm straddled a stretch of Sunday Creek. In that place my husband and I liked to sit on the back porch making plans for the crumble down barn on our stretch of the banks. We thought it would be charmingly pastoral to hang one of the old charm signs over the hayloft. My favorite was the good luck distelfinke, which is a stylized bird with a red feather coming out of the top of his eye that makes you think of quail. There is a curving fretwork of blue feathers down his neck like an echo of fish. The wings are a yellow plumage of jagged lightning folded close against the body. He often perches atop a tulip that means faith but opens out petals like a kiss.

Like most everyone else in those coal boom turned depopulated and heroin-addled towns known as Little Cities of the Black Diamond, we found it hard to justify the expense of barn paint when we were being so carefully, anxiously strategic about groceries and gas. The basement was leaking and the heater had a troublesome rattle that echoed through the house.

A local conservation group hired my husband for minimum wage to be a water quality specialist, because he knew something about wildlife biology and something about lab work, and because once in another watershed another lifetime ago he lost the Ozark farm of his childhood to the lead mines, who owned the underground rights beneath his family's farm and sunk the water table during a bad drought summer. There was a spring next to the foundation of his great-grandfather's cabin that burbled up a little creek where the cows drank. That summer the water ran yellow and then it ran dry.

Sometimes our stretch of Sunday Creek ran silver and turbid and we did not know why, despite repeated phone calls to Buckingham Coal who still had a dig upstream. In Truetown, nine miles downstream of us the creek had long since turned orange and stank of rotten eggs because of a collapsed 19th century mine that allowed water and oxygen to mix with coal ash that was meant to have been locked inside the earth forever when the mines finished with it a hundred years ago. Gob piles lining the creek bed were a charcoal and tarry mess of barren sludge gone to stone.

Old timers said you could dunk your kid in the waters of that acid mine drainage, holding on tight to her ankles, to cure her of lice. It was the kind of spell you can find in *Long Lost Friend* beside suggestions for stinging nettles, which are "Good for Banishing Fears and Fancies, and to Cause Fish to Collect." The book promises, "Whenever you hold this weed in your hand together with Millifolia, you are safe from all fears and fancies that frequently deceive men." It goes on to say, more practically, "If you mix it with a decoction of hemlock, and rub your hands with it, and put the rest in water that contains fish, you will find the fish to collect around your hands." I read this to Brian on a day when he came home sweaty and broke-down tired after dragging a 100lb generator through a mile of brush to reach the creek where they sent voltage through the water to shock the fish. Momentarily stunned, the creatures bob to the surface, where the scientists record their paltry numbers and the distressing absence of certain key indicator species, before they flicker back to life and disappear beneath the murk once more. If only he had known it could be so much easier, he says, stretching his sore arms out behind his back.

Here is a remedy to be applied when anyone is sick. "Let the sick person, without having converse with anyone, put water in a bottle before sunrise, close it up tight, and put it immediately in some box or chest. Lock it up and stop up the keyhole; the key must be carried in one of the pockets for three days, as nobody dare have it except the person who puts the bottle with water in the chest or box." There are no instructions about what to do at the end of three days. Drink the water? Pour it down the drain? Forget you ever put it in that box in the first place?

I wonder how clear the water was running or how long it had been left in its dark box when John Blymire went to see Nellie Noll, who everyone called The River Witch. According to the newspaper reports from that terrible summer in 1928, it was The River Witch who told him he needed a lock of Nelson Rehmeyer's hair and a copy of his spell book to burn in order to lift the curse of his hard life. First he scouted out the Rehymeyer place by pretending he was a hungry hobo. Rehmeyer gave him lodging that night and fed him breakfast in the morning. He poured him coffee and passed the syrup. Blymire came back the next night with two teenage accomplices, 14-year-old John Curry and 18-year-old Wilbert Hess.

There is a remedy you can use when anyone is falling away, and which, the book swears, has cured many persons. "Let the person in perfect soberness and without having conversed with anyone, catch rain in his pot, before sunrise; boil an egg in this; bore three small holes in this egg with a needle, and carry it to an ant hill made by big ants; and that person will feel relieved as soon as the egg is devoured."

Where we lived there was no talk of river witches or Nellie Noll. There was only Mountain Mary and her legendary goodness. With her hands alone, the old timers said, she could heal you. But all you can find now of Mountain Mary is her name. It's on a forest here, a wet weather ditch there. There are crumble down cabins in the way-back woods people will say must have once been hers.

Those who know well the spells in *Long Lost Friend* say she would have saved you with these words from Ezekial:

> And when I passed by thee and saw thee polluted in thine own blood, I said unto thee when thou wast in thy blood, Live; yea, I said unto thee when thou wast in thy blood, Live.

They say she was something powerful good in the midst of these terrible hard hills, they say she walks them sometimes still like a sweet wind looking to brush past your hair and make you alright.

There is a mist every morning that fills up the hollers so thick you can hardly see, and then there comes a moment each day when you crest a high ridge and see the sun all of a sudden fully risen. You can look down the valleys and see the red and white barns, some of the very fine ones decorated by a large painted quilt square or one of the many hex signs. A red horse head in silhouette protects animals from disease and the barn from lightning. A maple leaf brings contentment, oak leaves are for strength. Often the two signs interweave in a sunburst of fortitude and happiness. Raindrops are a call-down promise of fertility for the soil and the family.

On other days there is that other haze, the one still smoking out of the earth, ever since 1884 when miners in New Straitsville had been striking hard against the poverty, the exploitation, and the dangerous working conditions. When the owners brought in scabs, the miners slipped into the coal seams and started a fire. By the time anyone who might have stopped it realized what was happening, the underground was blazing and a hundred years later it's still burning, smoke still escaping through sinkholes to the surface every now and again. The mixture of defiance and righteous indignation cutting against the unforeseen consequences of foolhardy violence seems sometimes like the truest story this place knows how to tell about itself.

That was an old mining disaster, but there keep on being new ones. Every time an old dig collapses, a new fountain of sludgy mess springs out of the ground. The Upper Big Branch Mine Disaster was in 2010 and 29 people died digging coal out from beneath a West Virginia mountain. It still hangs heavy on our minds and the minds of our neighbors.

The spell to prevent conflagration is a long and complicated affair involving a black chicken, a piece of shirt worn by a chaste virgin and cut off according to her own terms, an egg laid on a Thursday, wax, pots, and various days of burying things beneath the threshold. Another method of stopping fire is to say these words:

> Our dear Sarah journeyed through the land,
> having a fiery hot brand in her hand.
> The fiery brand heats, the fiery brand sweats.
> Fiery brand, stop your beat.
> Fiery brand, stop your sweat.

Long Lost Friend is the kind of book where "beat" is perhaps a typo and should read "heat" or perhaps is exactly what the author intended. Among the dozen ways to stop bleeding, one is to say these words:

> I walk through a green forest;
> There I find three wells, cool and cold;
> The first is called courage,
> The second is called good,
> And the third is called stop the blood.

I have gone and will go to many public hearings. I know the spell "To Gain a Lawful Suit." I know you take large leaves of sage and write the names of the twelve apostles on them, then put these in your shoes before entering the courthouse. Nevertheless, our little town and all of our neighboring towns took "donations" of the new coal ash the companies were otherwise required by law to dispose of as hazardous waste and used the flakes instead of salt on the roads in the winter. So with spring thaws new coal ash ran off the sides of roads directly into the creeks and we didn't even have to wait for some new disaster to turn another spring orange.

Nevertheless, treatment plans for the worst acid mine drainage sites were proposed. And time after time city councils voted the plans down. Once because the acid neutralized the wastewater they dumped directly into the creek, as they had no sewage system. Another time because the passive treatment ponds full of water reeds and other plants that would filter the toxins through their roots would not look as sightly as a smooth mowed lawn. Other city councils voted plans down because they didn't trust scientists and they didn't trust conservationists and they didn't trust people with nothing more to show for themselves than pride in all their degrees and accomplishments come to tell them what to do.

During these public hearings the earth began to shake as fracking destabilized the balance of bedrock and shale beneath our water table. Mountain tops were removed. We asked ourselves if orange water weren't the least of our worries and we knew the answer was simply that we had too many worries.

What happened to Nelson Rehmeyer is that no spell book could be found anywhere in his house or on his property. So the two men and the 14-year-old boy bludgeoned him, bound him to a chair, and set him on fire while he was still breathing. Despite being doused in kerosene, the body did not completely burn, which investigators said was one of the truly horrific things they'd ever seen.

What happened to Nelson Rehmeyer is that he gave food and shelter to the people who would slaughter him, to people who did not know how to know a blessing when the plate was handed to them.

What happened is this. When an old woman dies, she is dead, her cabin crumbles to the ground, and she's not around anymore to put her hand on your cheek and tell you it's going to be alright. When you light an old man on fire, whether he be some old witch or the spirit of a mountain or just a kind and generous bachelor, now he is dead too. There is nothing that is going to change that.

Long Lost Friend is a broken book. A support beam cracked, the roof collapsed, the water poured in or the fire did, the tailings and the ash everywhere. Now no one dares drink from the poison of those pages. It has spells to make divining rods, spells to life a curse, spells for mending. I wish I believed it could do us any good.

> To Mend Broken Glass: Take common cheese and wash it well, unslaked lime
> and the white of eggs, rub all these well together until it becomes one mass,
> and then use it. If it is made right, it will certainly hold.

Translation Folio

CARSTEN RENÉ NIELSEN

Translator's Introduction

David Keplinger

ONE OF THE FIRST CARSTEN René Nielsen poems I translated, now almost twenty years ago, was a little gem called "X-Ray":

> She uses the tail of a fish skeleton as a fan. Musical tones pour out of her ears and float through the air like droplets; it is a room with no gravity. She dances slowly in place with her three most important tubes: the spine, and the windpipe, and the arms, which work as a balancing rod. Together they form three white lines in the dark. Her face is not seen.
>
> (from *World Cut Out with Crooked Scissors* [New Issues, 2007])

Hundreds of poems later, and now well into our third collection together, Nielsen's poems still alarm me—or rather, align me—with my mysteries. Like the figure in the x-ray, the most important tubes of my own body go about their balance-work with little help from the head, or from the face, or from most of the surface images by which I am judged. I also pass my judgements on others; meanwhile the rest of me, much to my own ignorance, goes on dancing at some gamma level of the unconscious. In *World Cut Out with Crooked Scissors*, his selected works in English, we anthologized Nielsen's collections, *Cirkler* ("Circles" 1998), *Clairobscur* ("Chiaroscuro" 2001) and *Enogfyrre dyr* ("Forty-one Animals" 2005). Later came the slim volume, *House Inspections* (BOA, 2011). We are at work on a companion translation to *Enogfyrre dyr*. *Enogfyrre ting* ("Forty-one Objects") was published in his native Denmark in 2017. The poems in this portfolio were completed in Berlin later that same year.

In my courses on literary translation my students seek out international poets and engage in the same type of collaborations. The collaborative act is one of simultaneous engagement and removal. While you are the vehicle for this work in the new language, you have to be like the skin of the woman in "X-Ray," where only the barest bones of influence shine through. And your face must not be seen. Nevertheless, it was because of this work with Nielsen, begun in 1997, that, ten years later, I was hired at a university in the East to teach poetry writing and literary translation. There is something beautiful about the unexpected returns of this work. It would seem that the more invisible one tries to be, the more the benefit to one's own art and one's own life.

What is the object of translation? There seems to be a distinct object for each translation. To force a pun, there are forty-one objects, one for each poem in his fine, new collection. I have said elsewhere that the aim of this work is to build the perfect, idiomatic and musical habitat so the translation can "survive in captivity." Thus for each poem a slightly different environment. For each object, a form fitting box. But now I think I was wrong about captivity. It is the poem that must captivate; it must become bigger than itself if it is to live in the new language. The magic work of the poet (and the translator) is to convince the reader that there is a mental space they already have reserved for this strange experience. And then the poem throws its butterfly net over them.

Born in 1966, Nielsen lives in Aarhus, Denmark's second largest city. It is a bit of a Boston to Copenhagen's New York. But smaller, more compact. A Jutlandish city, it prides itself on its removal from the urban center. So, while Nielsen's poems are surrealistic, he has stripped them of ornamentation, ostentation, and over-experimentation. Many of the recent poems read like folk tales in some strange Dictionary of Objects. They are prose poems in the lineage of Francis Ponge and Max Jacob. His influences, in fact, are all Surrealists, Dadaists, or French Symbolists—Hans Arp, Benjamin Peret, and Magritte among them. Many of his influences, too, are American: Charles Simic's *The World Doesn't End*; Joel Brouwer's brilliant *Centuries* (Four Way Books, 2003); Mark Strand's *Almost Invisible*, and the prose poetry of James Tate and Russell Edson.

In fact, it should be of little surprise to us that Nielsen's strangeness has been embraced—perhaps more than in Denmark—in the United States. His books have found a following here where a cerebral, Pythonesque silliness stands a chance to draw a crowd. Nielsen's archeological excavations, with its grown men in baby carriages, spider theaters, and sneezing trumpets, serve as antidote where politics have sickened us: the delusion of self-importance is momentarily washed away, and a clown sings from inside his barrel, rolling down a dark and lonely street.

CARSTEN RENÉ NIELSEN : Five Poems

Diary

Throughout an entire year, in 1963, my father recorded in his pocket calendar when he went to bed and got up in the morning, when he took a shower, whom he had coffee with, and what he saw on television. Nothing was too insignificant or mundane to be mentioned. Over the course of several days, you can follow the problems surrounding the purchase of a cord for his tape recorder. He often loses at badminton, buys a pipe, takes the bus to Aarhus. Only one brief mention of the assassination of John F. Kennedy in November ruins the impression of an almost perfect narrative: uninterested, fragmented, incomplete.

Pants

It has gotten too hot in these pants. I have to take them off and get into her pants instead. It is in her pants that the essential questions are asked. What is the sound of a bicycle rusting in a garden shed? Were we ever boating in a red canoe? Is the locomotive still standing in the public pool? Who has woken up the towels? So much one doesn't understand. Nevertheless there is always some fool who seeks an answer. "Towards North, constantly towards North," is mumbled despairingly, somewhere out there in the darkness of the pants.

Ruler

Every morning we were given lessons on how to tie knots. The Grauballe Man's Knot was certainly the most difficult. Later we were shown the withered pinky toe of Saint Eisenhower and told to measure the size of each other's skulls. We were very envious of the upperclassmen who had already received their machine guns. I had a clear feeling that the teachers didn't tell us the whole truth, but like all children I just tried to defend my place in the hierarchy. There were just four inches down to the bottom.

Grand Piano

Following the birth he was laid out in a grand piano. He lived fairly well off his wordless daydreams and by the few faint notes the strings produced when he turned in his sleep. Outside on the street, people passed with black umbrellas, the streetcars full of snow stood parked in the cemeteries, zeppelins hung attached to the sky by pins. Had the moon crumbled into the fine dust that settled on his eyelashes? Did the sun rise in his right ear and set in the left? Did he have any siblings, and well, who was that, who every year on his birthday sat down at the piano and began to play, but always stopped so suddenly and without any explanation?

Pillow

The pillows were so big and soft, our heads disappeared into them when we went to bed in the guest room at night. As we fell through clouds within the pillows, little by little we noticed the small differences. From one cloud white hairs were growing. On another lay a letter. You saw something blue. I saw the cut-out dolls. Any moment now, we imagined that the last cloud will have been reached, and a vast sundrenched landscape will open up beneath us. But we got wiser. We are still in the pillows, and the days become years like this, while we plummet, cloud after cloud.

translated from the Danish by David Keplinger

AMY STUBER

People's Parties

1.

ON THE LAST DAY OF 9th grade, Beatrice found herself at a rooftop party in The Mission. It wasn't the kind of thing she normally did: friends, groups, music. Someone was playing "Jessie's Girl" on repeat, and people in gold tennis shoes and embroidered bomber jackets and overalls were dancing and hugging and then dancing again.

It was a moment. Beatrice could appreciate it from a distance: the irony and the glee all wrapped together like a snow globe that someone kept shaking and shaking. After thirty minutes, she went down the hatch in the roof, down the spiral staircase, and into the apartment owned by the boy having the party. The boy, Frederick, was a junior, and both his dads did something in tech, and it was clear they cared about their apartment. Heath pottery in careful stacks on the raw wood kitchen shelves. A charcoal velvet couch, the requisite art books in their official towers. Hanging plants on delicate wires making a garden out of almost every window.

Her hair had been long then, to her waist almost with the bottom inches of the brown dyed black, and she'd let her grandmother Wendy cut bangs that had immediately developed a mind of their own so that she'd had to shellac them with coconut oil before leaving her house. She assumed they now just looked wet and would elicit a forehead-wide patch of acne.

There was this presumed promiscuity of everyone her age. Her mom Ray's friends liked to talk about it in the way of, "Bea I'm sure all your friends are hooking up already, so just be careful." One: she didn't have friends. Two: no one had so much as kissed her, and she was fine with that. She was a fan of boundaries. She'd seen what it meant to be a girl in 2017, and she had chosen to dismiss it wholeheartedly.

So it was with caution, disbelief, and a little bit of oblivion that she met Frederick's attention. In the two dads' bedroom, beneath the noise of the party, she'd hidden out on a corner loveseat, door to the bedroom almost closed, and made a show of flipping through a Vivian Maier book, just to seem occupied should anyone else venture down from the roof. She had practiced staying off her phone on such occasions. She didn't want to be one of those girls always on her phone. As a point of protest, she did not Snapchat.

And Frederick's progress was slow: first peeking in the bedroom and giving her a small wave, then making an ice water in the kitchen (she heard the clatter and plunk), then returning to the bedroom, pointing and fake laughing at his Bernie shirt onto which he'd Sharpied a giant "I told you so," then clicking the door closed, and picking up another art book (William Eggleston) and still not saying anything, then sitting on the edge of the bed and saying one thing while looking down ("Sick pictures. Totally relevant, still") and then a full thirty seconds later looking up to see if Bea was listening or looking, then sitting beside her but separated by whole inches of fabric for a full half-hour of parallel reading before he really went in. She could practically feel the weight of people's feet on the roof some fifteen feet above them, but the music was muffled by the closed windows and door. He was so quick and she was so unsuspecting that she couldn't find her voice, couldn't for the life of her even remember the word no. Instead, she stared for those few minutes at the open Vivian Maier book that had fallen on the floor, at one bleak and disarming picture of an elderly woman in a hair net and a fur coat, the sun making its spotlight a dagger on the fur, and the woman's face saying to Bea: this is all your fault.

Later that night in the bathroom of the house she shared with her mother, she used a pair of kids' safety scissors and a pink plastic razor to disarm her head of all its hair. She slept with two ragged stuffed animals pressed into either side of her face and did her best from the following morning forward to pretend the night had never happened.

2.

THE HOUSEBOAT IS full of women, many of them draped in ponchos from other continents. Ray, in a yellow '60s coatdress and gold clogs, leans into her girlfriend Chantal on a giant sheepskin in the houseboat's central room. Through the boat's front window, Ray sees her daughter Beatrice sitting on the front railing and reading *The Nation* under a tiny outdoor light. The party—Chantal's 40th—is a mix of vegan appetizers, the usual lesbians, Tequila rickeys, and an improvised game of Trivial Pursuit wherein every answer is changed to a horrifying fact about Donald Trump. It is too easy.

When Ray slept with anyone anymore, it was with women. She'd learned after 40 that she preferred it, the tits, the sway, the languidness. She was a small woman, bony and just five feet, and she was attracted to big women, fat women even. In the past ten years, her friend group had morphed from moms she knew through Bea's various Montessori and Waldorf schools to a handful of exes. Now when they gathered for their endless Friday night dinners, she felt like Joan Didion standing around at a Weight Watchers meeting.

Ray had finished an architecture degree in the mid-'90s and had at the time many ideas about communal and portable housing. She'd spent a summer in Malawi building structures out of reclaimed materials and helping a Scottish guy install solar panels in clinics. In the second half of her 20s she scrapped it all and played with a band whose punkish skater singer appealed to a large number of disgruntled white boys. She'd slept with many of them, and one of them—she'd never known which one— was Bea's father.

The first year of motherhood was unbearable. Ray's own mother, Wendy, a musician, a nomad who had raised Ray in VW vans and lean-tos up and down the north coast, had vanished a month before Bea was born and had only resurfaced after Bea's 10th birthday.

Ray spent Bea's first year on welfare and living in one room in a basement near The Mission. She and Bea slept on a single mattress, and she often ate from dumpsters. Her music friends either didn't understand her or wanted nothing to do with her. One night one of them brought her a puppy ("I thought it would cheer you up," he said) and Ray —out of her mind with sleeplessness—let the dog out the window and onto the sidewalk just before sunrise and never heard from it again. Ray, ripped open by insomnia, pushed a screaming or sleeping Bea down all the sidewalks late at night. Once after midnight, a stumbling man in gold pants stopped, pulled down his shining pants, and peed into the open stroller, right onto Bea's blanket. There was nothing more alone feeling than being alone outside with an infant at 2 AM. Once Bea turned one, Ray got her into a HeadStart daycare and found a temp gig at an architecture firm where she eventually worked her way up to designing kitchens for tech industry moms who all wanted the same thing but swore up and down they were nonconformist and interesting.

Chantal's houseboat kitchen was a jungle. The butcher's block table under the window was covered entirely by plants, their tendons spilling over the wood. Thirty small plants hung from the ceiling in macramé hangers, and she had so much jasmine that the smell gave Ray a headache. Chantal kept a watering record on a wall calendar with tiny checkmarks, one for each plant, "because they know if I don't check them off," she'd once told Ray. Ray hated magical thinking of all kinds, but Chantal was the mother she'd never had: soft, a hugger, someone Bea would actually speak to even when she wasn't speaking to Ray.

At the end of Chantal's party, a large boat passes too close in the bay, and the houseboat rocks as if it's out on open water. One stoneware dish full of picked-over wrapped figs slides off the table and crashes onto the floor where it takes on the look of carnage. The glass of red wine Ray is holding sloshes up onto her dress. Bea comes running in the sliding door. A few years before, Ray and Bea had watched a documentary about a teenaged girl who sailed around the world by herself, and Ray remembered Bea wanting so badly to be that girl.

The water smooths out, and the boat settles. The women throw the broken plate into the trash and wrap themselves with bags and scarves to head back to the city. Ray looks down and sees what looks like a South America of red wine traveling down the front of her dress. Chantal throws one of her many geometric print coats over Ray's shoulders, kisses her, and Bea and Ray are out the door.

After 40, Ray had donated almost all her clothes, anything patterned or fussy, and started from scratch, scavenging at the Goodwill in the Haight. She'd gone mono-chromatic. All blue on one day, all white on another. And she'd stopped watching men. She'd stopped reacting to their reactions to her. She'd reached an understanding of their fundamental envy of women, their lifelong power grab. It made sense to her that Donald Trump grabbed at women's pussies. It was the one thing he could never really have. That power of breath and push, the power of having a life in her life and then releasing it. All the business suits in the world, all the Morgan Stanley men, all the tech industry dudes with their child playground workplaces, all the men who had prodded her and catcalled. They had had her, but they didn't have her anymore.

On the way back down to the city, Ray drives slowly over the bridge. "Remember that movie about the girl on the sailboat," Ray says to Bea, and Bea says nothing but nods and points out to the water where there appear to be hundreds of boats of all sizes, their lights creating broad yellow planets of the water around them. It is like this with them now, and Ray finds herself giddy in these tiny allowed moments of connection. She grabs Bea's hand, and Bea, for several whole seconds, does not pull away.

3.

EVEN THOUGH SHE had once written a famous song that wrapped 1970s love in a package to hand out to teenagers in Iowa and Vermont and North Dakota who were cold and in need of dreaming, Wendy doesn't play music anymore. She is 70 and has lost her voice to smoking, and her fingers hate the guitar.

Instead, she wakes early and before heading to the beach to meet her daughter and granddaughter, she walks the neighborhood for at least an hour wearing massive gold headphones, a gift from her granddaughter Beatrice. She traverses the blocks to the beach, by all the noodle shops, the men smoking by trash cans, the ravens carving meals out of discarded plastic food containers, the trains ziplining their clatter down streets' centerlines. The whole neighborhood weighted with fog and metal feels poised to slip right off into the water. She missed the entire first decade of being a grandmother, and she's played her best catch-up since returning to the city.

Like all the mornings in the Outer Sunset, it is foggy. The usual swimming men sit near the water on their usual blanket, the one with a picture of a growling bear that looks 3D and almost velvet. As she does every Saturday, Wendy watches as the swimming men sit through a few final moments of observation before being stripped to nothing by the cold ocean water. The beach is uncrowded and chilly. There are a few teenagers camped out under a shelter built of driftwood and old towels. A group of mothers with children in layers of fleece try repeatedly to light candles on a birthday cake, but the wind keeps taking the flame, and then one of the kids scoops the center out of the cake and shoves the yellow into his mouth. Wendy hums low under her breath, a seashell tone, and looks at where water and sky come together in a gray line crosshatched by gulls and pelicans.

The swimming men rest metal coffee mugs on their bare stomachs, and in nothing but their swimming trunks and with the bellies of men years past middle age, they look pregnant. They are all her age, in that gauzy time of life when caring about others' opinions becomes less consequential. She has heard women complain about their invisibility after 60, as in "No one even notices me anymore," but Wendy delights in it. She wears whatever she wants. Sometimes she doesn't respond at all when a man asks her a question but holds his stare before turning away.

She watches as the bulldozer operators, three of them about a hundred yards down the beach, move and flatten the sand. Under her bed, she has a box that contains three records she made in her 20s, all with photos of her on the cover: one with hair to her waist standing in a field, smoking, another of her lying on a bed with a Moroccan scarf over her breasts, and another where she floats on her back with a daisy behind each ear in a perfect '60s kidney-shaped LA pool. When she thinks back on that time, she can only remember her physical self, the body, but she can't remember what it felt like to be that person.

The bulldozer operators take a break and gather by the steps, circulating a flask. They drink and then lean against the retaining wall where someone has spray painted "Deport Trump" in rainbow bubble letters and an abstract monkey in purple shouting: "Bananas for the People!" The sun makes a line on the beach and quickly disappears, and she has a second during which she feels like she is hovering above herself.

She sees her daughter and granddaughter on the steps. Her daughter is all in white like Yoko Ono. Her once-black hair is now half gray and in braids. Bea's short hair is covered in a thick black wool hat, and she looks in all directions in the way of a mouse spotted out in the open by a human.

This is their Saturday ritual now. Ray brings an old-timey picnic basket with her and positions herself cross-legged on a blanket next to Wendy so that she never really has to look at her. They are still in this holding pattern wherein Ray tolerates Wendy, and they never talk of the past. Bea lies on her stomach and eats peanut butter and honey toast, the peanut butter leaving prints on her cheeks that she doesn't bother to wipe away. Life astounds Wendy in a gut-punch kind of a way. The fact that she sits each Saturday on the beach with her tiny family of women she didn't know much at all five years before, no matter what the conflict or complications, is something.

When the swimming men set down their coffees and run to the water, their legs look part amphibian and part cadaver. The seagulls guffaw and scatter. The pastel houses hang on the cliff, almost but not entirely grayed out by the fog, and the green edge of the park carves a straight line into the flipped-ribbon chaos of the city.

The way the swimming men run without care is beautiful to Wendy. She never runs like that anymore, can't remember having run like that for years, but on this day she gets up and runs right after them just to the edge of the water, which is alive with shiny discarded mussels and fragmented crab shells. She watches the backs of the swimming men's legs as the water takes over their bodies, and then she herself drops face down into the sand, burrows herself full length in until she has sand even in her teeth. When she hears her granddaughter yelling her name, she stands up and turns around, and there is Beatrice, shoes off and running through the sand. When she reaches her, Beatrice, though 15, jumps up into her arms like a baby.

JONATHAN WEINERT

The Story of My Life

It has to do with the shape of a cloud
And the color of rain light
And the fog running its long tongue over the grass

To go fully into the cloud
To go fully into the rain
To go fully into the grass

Mom
I'm going
Dad

•

I held my teddy bear in one cold hand

A delicate translucent bubble swirled with primrose and crimson
Drifted over the grass
I watched it stretch and thin and rupture
Surrendering its crumb of soap

•

A shadow came straight out of a pine tree
As bright as daylight in the daylight world

Shadow firehounds moved in the shadow
And accepted my presence as a feature of the presence

I loved their indifference
How they didn't look up from sniffing the blinding grass

How they didn't hurry or scare as I always scared

•

Human bone makes a net of shadow
And the brain nests its meager light atop it

Which is the way I saw it
From the limb of a pine

•

A lake that once showed the face of a meadow
A meadow that once showed the face of a lake

Dead pines driven through the mat like splinters of whitegray bone

I could see where the shoreline once inscribed its sentence along a bank
All crazed and dried up now

A kingdom for milkweed and lichen and spider and mold

The wind rolled down from an invisible peak
And shook yellow powders from the ragwort and ivory fibers from the milkweed

I could see the dark inherent in the noon
The implied twilight

•

Some clock other than the kitchen clock
Advanced its hands of bone
And in that time
I could see the shadow
That never left the surface of the world

Who could I tell
My eyes grew huge with seeing
And my mouth held words
That nobody could understand

•

In the library always a book would say
Something like what I couldn't
But then it would veer away
Into character and plot

I wanted to stay with the dawn light rising over Indiana hills
And the horizons of rounded shadows sweeping the valleys
When the boy and his sister entered the rocket ship
Standing out in an abandoned airfield

Not the launch or whatever came after
Which I now forget
But the color of the light and the long shadows

And the quiet that surrounded the ship

MICHAEL PONTACOLONI

Neutral Buoyancy Laboratory

There is no anti-gravity chamber
at Space Camp,

though at a bar years later
I practiced being weightless

when my brother told a woman
she looked just like Pocahontas.

He threatened driving shell-eyed
to the strip club. I drove us both.

There is no anti-gravity chamber
at the strip club, but it's

the closest thing we've got my brother said
as he handed over twenty dollars

to buy me a lap dance. My undershirt
glowed in the ultraviolet

and ropes of pink light
circled the floor and the ceiling and

the stage. And in the blue plywood booth,
trembling like the universe,

I understood that God
is a subwoofer, that every astronaut

learns to listen underwater
and in the plush cabin

of a nosediving plane.

EMILY SKAJA

Dear Emily

Easy to disown the girl you were
at 23: fluffed dove-gray

& bridal, eyes up, prim bird claws
pink on the brute arm

of your first wreck,
your original lesson

in leaving a fire
to burn itself to ash.

With him you were cob-eyed,
blind-cut—a tin girl

ridged & perfect,
yawning flora,

all vinegar
hysteria & brine.

So you dreamed
that he drowned

you. You dreamed of blue
floodwater mold,

the traps he set
wire by hook.

You waited for hail,
a plague of swollen fish

to sting his mouth
before you slapped him,

before he told you
You're the one

who ruined your life.
You knew

all the reasons,
the ledgers, the birds

caught in windows,
your hands flaking rust—

tin girl clutching what,
holding what

to hide your nakedness?
Give her up now, that girl

who can't be you,
who can't be anyone

flung over his bed
like a sheet.

KATHLEEN McGOOKEY

The School of Anguish

Scarred wooden desks line up in rows. Miss Valenetti wears red heels and a clingy yellow dress. We may not say she looks like a volcano or sunset or fishing lure. Instead of spelling, she tells us last night's dream: she dove through a hole in the ice to retrieve matches chained to a cinder block. She couldn't open the box. We may not say our dreams or ask questions about that stubborn box. In gym class, we sit in a circle while Mr. Tully unties our shoes and cries. Then he ties them again. We don't even play duck duck goose. At lunchtime, the cafeteria ladies scoop boiled tongue onto our blank trays.

The Haunting

They lived with the ghost of the old boyfriend who only appeared in mirrors and haunted the perimeters of rooms, glowering and pouting against the walls. He never said a word but watched her daughters eat dinner, carry their plates to the sink, and open their notebooks. He watched her practice stain removal in many forms. Their sweaters shrunk. They grew out their hair. Her daughters looked just like her. The new man wore flannel shirts and took care of sheep—unusual in this day and age, but he liked the outdoors. She called him in when smoke filled the house. The ghost unsettled visitors, whether they could see him or not. If asked about a chill or flicker, she'd say, *That's just David, my old boyfriend from Europe.* Sometimes he loitered at the window and let moonlight illuminate his face. Or he gazed into the foggy dawns, pretending to see an airplane glinting as it approached snow-capped mountains. His loyalty, though misplaced, had become a point of honor. In the early days, she ordered him to leave, burned juniper, and hung a wreath of blackberry and ivy on her door. They moved and moved again, and he always came along. She hardly ever wondered how to say *feather* or *cloud* in French. She guessed she was not the first person to live this way.

CHRISTOPHER KEMPF

Senior Night

They hand their mothers roses. They know this
means they are men now, & indeed the girls
in the bleachers tonight, their faces—each
high, hot cheekbone—embellished, I do not
fail to notice, with tiny bulldogs, love
most, the girls do, the boys' new muscles. Touch
of pelt on the upper lip. & with what
strict detachment they attend, the boys—blind,
they suggest, to the night's ceremony—
to their free-throws & layup drills, as if,
for instance, the intricate ritual
of the wheel-route were, for them, exercise
in those solemn maneuvers of war sport,
we know, began as. On the playing fields
of Eton, Waterloo was won. In bogs
surrounding the courts at Chichen Itza
excavations, papers say, have turned up
rubber balls bands of Mayan warriors
hip-checked through limestone hoops. Or who,
sometimes, used the heads of their victims. This
is Ohio though, the suburbs. For us
the forced march at Pendleton, & ready-
to-eats & gas masks & the flags first one
half the gym then the other comes to its feet
now to salute seem, I admit, mostly
distant if regal abstractions. Capital
is like that. While a boy in St. Clairsville
signs his name in some sad storefront the mall
rents cheap, his mother—& this image just
for the pity—beginning to weep, we
turn blithely to our night's great circus, its
cheerleaders' habits newly pressed, the pep
band's saxes glittering. A division

of labor, Marx called this, who understood
indeed that when they are finished splitting
& cutting toward the basket, & after
their sky-hooks & jump shots & their sweet—*sweet*
they will call them—crossover fades they will,
the boys, begin at last that long-held practice
of surrender. For Sunday rec leagues. Yes,
for girls become their mothers, & for Buicks,
& dogs, & double, flat-paneled monitors
on which, like men, they will let the market
run wild across the flatlands. Imagine—
the villagers fleeing. The flags raised one
by one, afterward, in the rulers' rafters.

CHRISTOPHER WARNER

Enhanced Interrogation Techniques

> I even have recurring nightmares that I'm in my cell at Abu Ghraib, cell 49 as they called it, being tortured at the hands of the people of a great nation that carries the torch of freedom and human rights. —Ali Shallal al-Qaisi

1.

I will make you dance, crow
I will make you hop upon my box
I will press upon you in the darkness
I will crush you like a wayward spark
smoldering in the thin grasses

2.

Black burlap scratching
cheek bones and chest hair.
The slap of skin on cold concrete.

When I screamed, I gave what you required.
When I wept, I gave more than was asked.

You ate it like an animal.

3.

Brothers, I did not know.
I did not know
you were alive like this.

FOURTEEN POETS

from

IRELAND

and the

UNITED KINGDOM

Introduction

DURING THE SUMMER OF 2017 I was in Belfast, Northern Ireland, where friends kept recommending poets in both the Republic and the United Kingdom. It turns out Belfast is an excellent vantage from which to catch a glimpse of British and Irish poetry! I started writing down names.

What follows is recent work by 14 Irish and UK poets, most of whom are not, I believe, particularly well known to the average American poetry reader.

It's important to say up front: This feature has no aspirations of aesthetic unity or exhaustive representation; it by no means offers a full or clear picture of what's happening "across the pond," nor does it intentionally advocate for any particular sort of poetry that's being written there. These are simply poets whose work Brian, Nicky, and I admired as we read through the writers who were recommended to us (and who *those* writers recommended, etc.) and who had some recent work available to send.

The oldest poets included here are about 50; the youngest are in their mid 20s (and the selection moves more or less from older to younger). Though two of the included poets live in Scotland, none are originally *from* Scotland—which is simply the product of how the feature came together (who responded to our solicitations, who had recent work available).

In the interest of clarity and ease for our primarily American readership, we have mostly Americanized spellings. The exception is in Sam Riviere's poem "In the Provinces," which is so consciously about "Britishness" that it seemed odd, in that case, to Americanize the presentation.

We are grateful to Culture Ireland for partial support of this project. And we are excited to present this group of poets from Ireland and the UK. We hope you find their work as eclectic, moving, and exciting as we do.

—Wayne Miller

CONOR O'CALLAGHAN

In Memory of the Recent Past

for Rachel Genn

Think of it like this:
if antiquity is
an elevation in silhouette
on the horizon,
and what we pause on
as one might a scenic overlook at evening
is present,
then past must form
the vale that falls between
in grades of recentness.
Most recent is nearest.
Too near to see,
it recedes from us as noise.
We hear it.

We mark it pending.
Not yet sufficiently distant
to laugh about,
it won't ask forgiveness
the way history does,
nor indulge us such indifferent ease.
Its dark age is more
the traumatic quotidian
of yesterday, the day before
we shared
and wish we hadn't,
the earth beneath our feet,
what happens
while we're speaking.

The recent past says *I want us back*
in the same breath
with *This can be undone*
(but never how).
It doesn't so much end
as discontinue
ad infinitum
at successive nows.
Its news is old,
if only just.
Its fruit, that looked so pretty
on the window sill
no one touched in months,
is wilting over.

Fly we wouldn't hurt
yet somehow did,
it haunts.
Its horrors are
of small hours.
It hurts itself.
We tell it, *We're so sorry.*
We confess,
It's your very only-just-ness
that's the killer.
It's made of stuff
we can't help making more of
with every second shed
like skins or love.

Just there, even,
in a place we're no longer.
You smiled. I smiled too.
As if we both could hear,
amidst us, a thing
that must remain implicit
to cling to living, dearly.
At the core of every waking moment
is slippage
so granular, so infinitesimal,

to be as near inaudible
as makes no difference.
We still hear it.
The trick is not to listen.

Upon the Very Nature of Loss

I return a fraction of myself. Five-sevenths?
A healthy fraction, but a fraction nonetheless.

What of that hip flask of remaindered flab?
Word has it it's—*he's*—been getting along famously.

Such irony! That fats burned on river tracks
to seem svelte, lovable, should club together, be so

loved by a population of greater Ulaanbaatar's worth
of friendship circle, prove even such a hit

with beached blubber at the bar of Big Jim's
beneath the iron viaduct we never enjoyed

when he and I were joined at the gut,
politic, continent with his wisdom pearls,

my walking parable, mon brotherless semblable,
mon proverbial drawer of lidless tupperware.

And bully for him, my decommissioned underbelly,
my displaced excess anti-matter gone alien,

slumming it off some or other dispensation's radar
sans green card or social security or paperwork

of any order, my lardy doppelganger,
my collapsible table, my fabulously popular surplus-

to-requirements blockbuster nom de plume
for whom one is thrilled—naturally—to bits.

Listen. If you lie one ear to the ocean floor
you all but hear the whale of a time he's having.

LORNA SHAUGHNESSY

Bishop's Quay

Easy to forget
that being young and poor
was no hardship, and wealth,
an abundance of time to share bodies
in cold, damp rooms that smelled of briquettes
even in summer.

       The Corpus Christi procession
passed within feet of our single bed.
We watched through a thin curtain
faithful shadows line the curb,
emerged at midday for tea and bread,
survived on a sinners' diet of cheese sandwiches,
pints, and tea in cafes that had newspapers.

One winter, I read George Steiner in the Public Library
while you rehearsed. And once, inexplicably then,
cried for hours in our favorite pub.

PAUL PERRY

Leonora's Violin

It is a tomato
If you say so or a flamingo
Or a whatnot
It is the laughter you gather at dusk
It is the talk talk
Guffaw and shush of the wind
It is the rain in a glass jar
Ha or the sun pooling at your feet
It is the sound of love
It is love too

VAHNI CAPILDEO

Everything Becomes Holy at Six O'Clock

everything becomes holy at six o'clock:
these triangular rooms, palomar ladder,
china shop candleholder, written guitar;
proud & sober, outdoor winter laundry lines.
jack's forbidden goyagraph stewed like cherries
in reheated cathedrals, my primesigned mind.
that girl's blush, posed with void replica armor.
ívar makes fire. he has six o'clock hands
for us, his old & borrowable children,
older than barbed habits, skyhook terminals.
the clock comes round again: six o'clock four times
today already; second-hand esquivel
wiped of dirt anointment; rough sleeper's greenery
tree baubled with street company. so he changed
his skull? he's a saint. c'est bizarre, comme train.
it isn't stopping, but it is making stops.
chris knows how everything becomes now, & when
sveinn must buy all the annunciations that are
colonnaded, must buy the colonnaded
annunciations at least once, maybe twice.
the christmas candle must be lit before
midnight. we are all going to hell. shells, pinecones,
silence horseshoed in toledo's synagogue.
sveinn carries north's unfiltered morning: someone
visiting a silhouette, pink, on dark green.
throughout i sought, sought & unfound, gifts for cats.
sveinn wants to spend a hundred days with his dog.

JAMES BYRNE

The Triumph of Fire

I unfold my handkerchief it is a flag.
—Aime Cesaire

Blood dries on the national rag.
Shadow gauze cuts your search
engine. Intel wipes you from the
register of international births.
You say goodbye before going,
mark west on the map of referenda.
Desiring of the locked door, ulcerous
as any subpoena, you are the hike
against centurial progress, the triumph
of fire. Strangeness of skin think,
your shit is unfertilized roses, your
v-finger on the channel hand.
Warm greeting in the freezer aisle,
we used to grunt at each other,
soon I will bump into you wearing
VR headgear. Utopic when occupied
by light, nervous in forest darkness,
you play is-was, clan-clash, check
the tyre mud in your driveway.
Coil tracks, snake prints, arched
screaming of a country choir.
The prayer inside your temple
spells DANGER in white ink.
Your speech sounds drowsy, as if
it were night, as if death meant
to smother a simple ending.

CHRISSY WILLIAMS

Casual Arousal in Murnau's *Faust*

Auntie is home, lapping
at the snub curved spout
of a love potion. Mephisto
peers into her parlor, grins,
flourishing a necklace of coins.
Auntie's coarse face delights
as he dances it behind her,
a spell, fastens it with lust,
reaches up under her arms
to smooth the money down
over her wide flat breasts
and holds them there.
Her smile is a discovery.
But. Mephisto withdraws.
He is not interested. She begs.
Begs. He pours a drink.
Mephisto grins again.
Auntie is beyond sin, here,
swaying desperation, wishing
more, and I am with her,
wishing now for everything.
Her hands search down
over thick skirts, below
her waist, pushing in,
her fingers an inverted prayer,
pushing the prayer further in.

Extract from Recovered Text Drafts

everyone loves a bassist in the muppets

hug is sexual remember when I press against you

do you want to talk to a dead or living

we are moving forward at the rate of history

apps are new wishes for children

my cock is also a promotional tool

what the fuck I swore you: tigers!

the written word has always persuasion

ELAINE FEENEY

Buy yourself a routine. Run like clockwerk.
Take the pills.

"I guess it wasn't exactly a triumph or anything, was it?"
—*Revolutionary Road*, Richard Yates

we were warned off the hell-hag routine by wise women who foresaw our
mornings boast at us & souring evenings, keeping us asleep for eight hours a

night, counting calories, clocking-up effort to our coffins, corset on our throats,
modulating cold earth for emptiness, once-upon-a-time-exploration-of-each-

other has been rerouted. my journeys to the Muckanaught mountains stopped.
just. like. that. dead end. dead stop. we synchronize to *fall pat* or *beseem* (word

son used yesterday) & we don't tell each other that we spend more time at
greasy filling stations for bags of Polish coal & pink donuts placed in brown

paper bags by pretty girls in fleece jackets who smell of gray tobacco & cola-
bubble-gum, temples not yet thistled-down by crows who leave a footprint,

(poem's title should be inserted here) so full up of hope for townie boys to come
buying lucozade and a Sunday breakfast roll & offer the last show in the IMC

that evening after the eleven shift, which they'll leave before the credits.

I've done those shifts.

where the clock moves backwards.

darling, I am chalking it out now on our kitchen blackboard, (if I can find chalk)
that if I am to highly resolve anything, (though I'm not taking up

space with such incrassate language), we are to avoid today, for a twenty-four
hour hesitation, let us drink gin for breakfast & curl my hair for ages and ages

like they do on YouTube channels before brushing upwards their eyebrows to
frame themselves. tonight, there is no supper. I will dine on you and we will light

the scatter cushions in two burning parallel rows, (we will of course check that
the inner filling isn't toxic to the children) I will drain the cleaning products

under the sink when my eyebrows are on fleek & use the leftover plastic to
sow cress and micro plants & Stefane's saved champagne will be brunch

accompanied by squid we order in, (though its not the first Saturday night of the
month) & we will order out lunch and eat for so long that we skip teatime

so I see the spark in your eyes, not the bags under them & the muscle
in your forearm will not remind me that you need to powerhouse the gables.

this is happening now. for we should see the wood for the trees and the trees
for the forest (we will hear the notes of a child chiming on a dead oak

branch but we will go to her when we are called, for she is laughing and bright &
not concerned for the dead tree, for she is alive & sings well unto midnight,

when we fall asleep from exhaustion). with you unshaven and me unshaven
& tongues of coffee, let our itchy fingers burn this house down & make four ash

angels on the front lawn, (when the ash cools), neighbors we never met will
bring us gifts, because that is their habit, (on the sorrowful backs of

others, to bring kindness), but we'll tell them that we're happy and gift them
ash in pickle jars to take home to their mantle places & to their shaker-side

boards & moonbeam-marble-granite tops & Xanax & codeine habits,
the clothes on our backs will be our hides like when we were young & fresh

with our bad habits and good music, when we went for days without sleeping
under a Spanish sun & to the night of the long birth, when routine was given out

to us, the helmsmen of our own making, in a Moses basket,
a whalebone-whack of prodigy & poison.

SAM RIVIERE

Regime of Signs

Out fetching lemons and cherries for sours

I encountered wan scenery in the doors of black cars

Driverless and low to the ground

Their grills laden with wreaths

And winking insignia

The whole cortege passing as a silent pageant

In the revolving lights of muted sirens

Transporting dead clergy

To a spireless crematorium

While in the parklands opposite

Surrounded by Irish grass and tough roses

A uniformed boy with a penknife gouged

Into a young tree the sacred heart and letters

As a girl looked on skeptically

Not yet impressed—

The sap that hardens

The superb gesture

In the Provinces

A few vague moths are trapped in the shade of the downstairs bathroom—the heat and cobwebs make it Greco-Roman. At the kitchen table, paranoid already, you peruse another feature . . . Seemingly blithe, the candidates man their grim devices and approach the deafening edge. June 2016: the Nespresso machine perforates its victims' lids with a hundred cuts, then drains their varied essences. Odours of chlorine and fluoride effervesce from tapwater. Ice dissolves to chalk-white sediment at the bottom of a glass. You speak as you shit—a sip of flavoured coffee sets you off in an inarticulate rush—then doze away the best hours, fully dressed, heavily diagonal, jolting awake like a faulty clockhand to watch flies bump against the detailed trees. The house is a hive of inactivity. Every half an hour someone announces 'Right!' and continues doing nothing. Then it's night: the moon, yellow and huge, peers across the fields at supper. Someone hoses flowerbeds under the alien glare . . . Later its full beam stuns you awake, risen high by three. Tomorrow a trip to the coast, Brexiteer country.

Thirty-six degrees in England! Typhoons or tornadoes from a recommissioned airbase worry at the barrier all afternoon; it flexes overhead, threatening to crack . . . On training runs, flying low, their landmark is a converted windmill. Once, crouching in the garden, you saw a squadron pass in diamond formation, silently heading east, for Saddam, and a second later their engines following—a country-wide reverberation. Almost sourceless, it filled the cloudless morning. Today they roll around the sky with a noise like coins scraping the insides of an old arcade machine, invisible for now, behind its neutral screen—but wait, there's one, the size of a gnat, banking north with insouciant haste . . . Surveying the dun-and-yellow plains of benign farmland, the hedgerows and pollen mist, or the tinselly arm of a sprinkler system, to them the English trees must look like citizens. There's less and less massed foliage, protecting rare, creaking forests, older than almost everything, territory of wasps and foxes: pagan species. Later warm raindrops pluck at the flowerheads, there's actual thunder.

ZOË BRIGLEY

Un/dressing Beatitudes

so dark & she hardly wore it because the color
was close but not close enough to a browner shade
the only consolation the sheen the dress had on winter
mornings or boat rides on a smooth, grey lake:
a horse's chestnut hide glinting gold and green

•

as easy & right as fitting
clean clothes with your first morning dress,
buttons snapped shut, stockings long
& taut against your legs, the seams
of your underwear matching the shape
of you: a heavy necklace on your chest
is a comforting hand

•

the comb in her hair becomes
a centipede, her compact
a turtle shell, the brush
for powder a great, soft
broom, & the glass
a fish bowl flashing

•

the folds were winged
but narrow as a hawk, fringes
like horse mane, a dress that blotted
the day, but cathedral tall, its skirts in full sail

•

in those Katharine Hepburn
high-waisted pants, the buttons
on the side stamped with an anchor
& chain, she sat
on the floor, cross-legged at the ankles, the long
loaves of her lace-up shoes: *I've never hit anything,*
she said, *that was in the right place.*

•

the little grooves pressed from the seams
of clothes onto skin are hardly perceptible, lines
crossing, pinking the flesh, present like a finger
tip against a forehead or chin:
its small, insistent presence

•

he forces her tiny shirt buttons out of each
slot, though they wedge in place, & it takes
the pressure of a finger, the counterweight
of a thumb to budge each one

•

bones fanning out, they expand from a flat
cage like an accordion's bellows, but without
the sound, & when the skirt drapes itself
over the wires, it makes a space round
the waist wide enough to tempt
a woman or man to reach across

•

the gold buttons themselves
like the heads of soliders, a helmet
pierced by a small black eye

•

the legs lengthen in her stockings, grow a shiny
second skin, the long seam at the back as if to say,
I know you're watching, I know what you can see

MARTIN DYAR

Flannery

Flannery was not a well-regarded vet.
Horse people tended to see straightaway
the fear his joking eyes sought to conceal.
Hating the roar of his jeep, cattlemen
spoke with flamboyant harshness when it passed.
Some swore his urban airs would bring a death.

Yet Flannery's business lasted five years,
the sore, elemental need of a vet
preventing us from venting face-to-face
the widely-held opinion that he was,
at best, a dogs and cats man who only
made farm calls out of vanity or greed.

Two brothers who'd spent countless hours online
researching ways of being vets themselves
(or close enough) met the locum in town.
And soon the story found a hundred lanes.
Flannery became an emblem of distress.
Authoritative slander was now hushed

in favor of fraternal commentaries
on what depression meant; on what women
could do to men's spirits by calling time
on a half love or, worse, on a true love
which, overnight, had ceased to anchor them.
Three counties wondered darkly in tandem.

A number said he'd butchered his own arm.
Most doubted this while echoing reports
of bandages and guards and hospital.
The girl he'd lost was readily recalled:
a wealthy type, a student who'd come west
on consecutive summers. With her wit

she'd left the gates of sentiment open
in many a yard when August bore her off.
Tonight, pub-mumbled empathies persist.
Words along the lines of, "Flannery neglects
himself. All vets, good and bad, are the same.
Most of them, mileage-mad, live without sleep.

And look, if livestock is not your calling,
and you're drinking (I heard he drinks alone);
if you're in workaholic territory,
and then a girl comes, a flower maybe,
a joker, and a better vet—well, look,
you're not a man at all if you stay strong."

JESSICA TRAYNOR

Photographing the Dead

Your father must have roved
his eyes about the room
during the long exposure,

past the photographer,
towards the clock on the mantel,
his hair askew, the motion

somehow hushing him.
Your mother would later think it
the cast of a lunatic.

Of course, she stayed rigid,
the halo of her movement
barely softening her edges,

her gaze glowering out of shot,
at the thought of tomorrow's
hard slog, or the worry

of arsenic in the wallpaper,
lead filings in the tea,
crinolines and open fires.

But you, at the center
of the scene, your eyes seek
something further afield

and the sideways shrug of your neck
suggests a nonchalance.
Your outlines are so clear

it is as if you are sloughing off
your dull-eyed parents
and entering the real.

I almost pity them, left behind:
all those years to fill with toothaches
and stillbirths, boils and cholera—

all that life shining
through their pasty faces,
and what are they to do with it?

STEPHEN SEXTON

O,

Earl Strickland I dislike you quite a lot
and it's not because you are a Gemini.

You skulk up to the table like a Gemini,
like a little god of diligence, fury,

and full-body English nine-ball breaks
but it's not really even that.

It's not the wrap-around sports sunglasses
or the pernickety quiver of break and game cues,

and hey, a belly is not unbecoming
for certain gentlemen of a certain age.

It's not the bristled trapezium
of your unmodish blond moustache,

it's not the cyan Lycra billiard glove,
chichi in the extreme, and less still

that weighted arm band fixed around your bicep
as an amulet or periapt. Whatever.

Earl, yours is a game for one played by two:
one of whom is you and the other, you.

From those regional pool halls eye-watering
with smoke, a bad moon often on the rise,

to the Riviera Hotel and Casino, Nevada
and the 8-ball Open sponsored by Camel—

you play in a long off-beat.
A gold tooth rattles down a drainpipe.

Earl Strickland I dislike you quite a lot
and not because you shellacked Stephen Hendry.

It's not the cues of cocobolo or rosewood
or who knows, the drawn and dressed neck and spine of a whooper swan

wrapped with stacked leather or Irish linen,
or the cotton you picked for pool money

on the farm in Roseboro, North Carolina;
and its tobacco, and its fat striped watermelons

rolling in the back of a pick-up truck
at angles you could, as a child, calculate.

Earl Strickland I dislike you quite a lot
for the junk of your regalia and your sneer.

Earl Strickland I dislike you quite a lot
for the beauty you achieve when beauty

is never your intention.
Earl Strickland, make like Pangaea and break.

Make like some ancient stage magician
who has cinched the trick so many times

he has finally forgotten how and when
the sleight of hand happens—

for whom it is a mystery the moment
a white handkerchief turns into a dove.

VICTORIA KENNEFICK

Corpus Christi Procession

That May
I collected
rose-heads
to peel off
their petals
and lay them deep
in my new wicker basket
lined with linen.
Dressed in white,
God's little bride,
I plucked out
each petal
and kissed it,
the Communion
wafer still stuck
to my palate.
Winding up
and down
the faithful hills
of Ballycotton,
I festooned the path
for priests to trample
all the petals brown.
I had been so careful
not to bruise them
with my lips.
Other girls sniggered
behind cupped hands,
whispered through
lacy fingers,
as my petals

rushed
to the ground
to die,
She's really
kissing them.

MANUELA MOSER

On writing about my grandfather

On photographs of Lotte

On Ernst Moser's doctoral thesis on the law of dowries and other forms of gifting "Die Mitgift"

On talking about conjecture with Robert

On the bank being taxed 86% by 1934

On Hans Rotolz

On the Schloss Ruhwald and Riefenstahl and the Olympics

On New York and why they didn't make it

On finding the video footage from the Mediterranean cruise they went on with credit from the unused tickets to New York

On how they dined out 40 years later on the remainder of the money

On Benjamin's *Berlin Childhood Around 1900*

On why there is so much memoir written about this period of time

On the unknowableness of it

On exile

On writing about an exile so long ago when there are so many in exile now

On a novelist saying that she will not write about the present because she does not see it as a subject

On the privilege of hindsight

On taking the privilege of hindsight for granted

On why some writers must write about the present and some about the past

On why some writers must write about the present because if they didn't there will be no documents to reference when writers write about the past

On how easy it is to make it all up

On whether that is truthful

On whether truth matters

On whether truth in writing matters

On whether truth in writing is the only thing that matters

On what truth is

On whether truth is objective or whether truth is subjective

On whether there is universal truth

On if there is a universal truth whether it is possible to write it or not write it

On whether what is subjectively observed and relayed is universal truth

On what is universally true

On watching an older poet and a younger poet talk about truth

On the older poet wanting to find truth and only that

On the younger poet not believing him

On watching this

On watchmakers

On notes from Peter's memoir

On Jewishness

On the difference between a nation and a state

On Jewishness being a mix of ethnicity, religion and nationality

On the two times Jews had political autonomy, once from 1350-586 BC, again from 140-37 BC

On the Jewish diaspora since 586 BC

On how Jews have lived as minorities in every country they live in except for Israel

On whether my family spoke Yiddish

On how the British government agreed to admit one thousand young survivors from the camps in 1946 but only 732 could be found

On how the first of these survivors went to stay in a hostel in Windermere

On the internment of Ernst and Claus and Peter

On Peter's real name

JACINDA TOWNSEND

Veneer

RUTH WAS TRYING HARD, SO hard, not to look at Clarisse Johns' legs, because she'd seen, when Clarisse entered the restaurant, that they were orange. Undeniably orange. Ruth couldn't decide whether it was a mistake of the wrong shade of pantyhose clashing with Clarisse's natural skin color, or a sudden inability on Clarisse's part to match her stockings to any other element of clothing, but either way it was an indicator of some sort of slippage, which might be a problem, since Clarisse was just coming off a two-week stint of psychiatric rehab.

Clarisse was Ruth's oldest friend on earth, the only person left who'd known her when she still had a brother. Ruth could never understand how it was that her family had suffered the consumptive tragedy but it was Clarisse who'd grown up and lost her mind: as far as she could tell, Clarisse had grown up in happiness, with a mother who sewed her dresses from McCall's patterns and a father who took her fishing every Saturday on his motorboat. Where Ruth had spent most of her fifth grade year watching her brother fester away in hospital after more serious and comprehensive hospital, Clarisse had still been secretly disassembling and reassembling her Lego Millennium Falcon. Clarisse had been popular with the boys in middle school and graduated third in their high school class: the worst time Ruth could remember happening to Clarisse was a school suspension for wearing a miniskirt.

Clarisse was pulling her hands into her shirtsleeves now, so far back that Ruth could see only her bitten-down fingernails. "Thanks for getting together," Clarisse was saying. "You know I cherish you."

"Same here," Ruth said, trying to put her hand over Clarisse's, but making contact instead with the top of her shirt sleeve. Ruth removed her hand and leaned back in her chair. "Feeling better?" she asked.

"I'm staying out of trouble, if that's what you mean."

"Not at all. It's not like you went looking for trouble."

"Yeah. It turns out even when you're not looking for it, it gets bored and shows up at your door."

The waiter came and wrote the orders of the table next to them, two couples who pondered the menu items and had a dozen questions they wanted answered before they would decide. Their accents came from a country that made them sound like vampires.

"What about you, Ruth? Things looking up?"

"I'm fine. I mean, my lawyer's costing too much money, but there's nothing worse than sleeping in a bed with someone who can't stand you."

"I still say he was joking."

"Baby. Darlin'. It was right there on his pass screen."

It had turned out to be literally true, that James hated her. He'd failed to kill his iPad alarm one day before an early meeting at work, and when it rang, at its full, bawling volume, Ruth had run into their bedroom to turn it off, but the device was locked and wanted a password. She'd typed in their daughter's name, *Annie*, as an educated guess, but the alarm continued its baying. *James1974* failed, as did *Cardinals* and *Hurly43*. She typed *Iloveruth*: the phrase failed in both lowercase and all caps. *Ihateruth*, she typed, as a joke. The alarm then went silent, blessedly silent. It had been so shocking that at first, she'd laughed.

Then she'd gone practical, checking all his open apps, scrolling through his gmail for further proof—correspondence with another woman, perhaps—but finding only Annie's homework notifications from school, unsigned ACLU petitions, and requests for his presence at a Kappa Alpha Psi mixer. She hadn't known what to do, but she'd known that her one and only phone call should be to Clarisse, and so Clarisse it was who, over the course of a fortnight, convinced her to file for divorce. "That, you don't need in your life," she said. "I hate Ruth? Fuck that. That pig. And all the shit you've done for his ass over the years? Take half."

"Jesus what's taking them so long," Clarisse was saying now, because the waiter had brought the vampires water and appetizers without stopping at Clarisse and Ruth's table. He'd even come back out with dinners for the table behind them, but again, he had not stopped, even when Ruth issued a timid "Excuse me?" at his retreating back. As always, she wondered whether it was because they were Black, or if their table was involved in some internecine restaurant labor dispute.

"I'm thirsty," Clarisse said. "I gotta take my pill."

"Fuck it then," Ruth said. "Wanna go?"

Clarisse giggled. "Whoa," she said. "Leave a man, you feel free to leave all kinds of shit. Yeah, okay. Let's Motorola."

They gathered their jackets and purses and got up from the table, and on their way out the door, the front desk hostess opened her mouth with all its various piercings to say something, but she didn't gather her thoughts fast enough to stop their progress, which was a relief. The door whooshed shut and they were outside in the vacuum of South Bardstown Road, the only available noise that of the spare car passing them by. The hard winter still bore down on the April air, and Ruth found herself buttoning her jacket, but Clarisse sang Eminem out into the cold. "You don't. Wanna fuck with Shady . . ."

"You. Are. Such a fool," Ruth said. "This is why we can't get served here in Lower Caucasia."

"Whatever," Clarisse drawled. She increased her volume until she was rapping at the top of her lungs.

She'd been like that, too, in the hospital where Russell was dying—Clarisse and her mother had shown up too later for visiting hours; Clarisse running across the hospital cafeteria where they'd been directed to find Ruth and her family; Ruth's mother then herself heavily medicated to ward off reality; her father awkwardly cordial and smiling with inappropriate affect; her older sister Wendy, she of the fraying cornrows, grown sour, worldweary, reckless with the boys at her high school.

Before Ruth could even stand, Clarisse was throwing both arms around her, pushing her sweater-encased body into a propulsive hug, knocking Ruth's bowl of hospital-grade chicken tetrazzini to the floor. "Jesus, I'm so sorry," Clarisse had said, as the plastic bowl clattered around the circumference of its rim.

"Watch the Jesus," Clarisse's mother told her. The bowl quieted itself.

Mrs. Johns gave her daughter a bunch of napkins and they both got down on hands and knees to wipe the smeared alfredo and chicken, stopping when a hospital custodian came with a mop. Even then, they quietly watched him work rather than resuming conversation, and Ruth knew they were grateful for the emergency of spilled food, because no one who visited Russell in the hospital ever knew what to say.

He'd been born sickly, her brother, spitting up his food even as an infant, tearing the ligaments of his ankle while performing normal childhood tasks such as playing dodgeball or jumping on a trampoline. At school, he peered through his thick glasses to decipher letter combinations he would never quite learn to decode. Their pediatrician, kind, cartoon-voiced Dr. Malone, had left the room one day after listening to Russell's heart at a routine appointment, only to come back fifteen minutes later with a referral to Jewish Hospital. Jewish sent Russell up the chain to Riley Indianapolis: Indianapolis sent him to Cleveland Clinic, where Ruth learned, sitting on I90, with her mother humming mournfully in the front seat, that traffic could move slowly enough for starlings to swoop down and roost on the median.

Nowhere in the Midwest, as it turned out, could anyone find an answer. "We must enjoy Russell as long as we can," her father said, one night after Russell turned up short of breath after a simple walk up the stairs and was sent to bed. "We can't possibly know how much longer we have with him."

Still, the end came with a vicious suddenness that surprised all of them, even her father. It had started after school on a Monday, a day Ruth relived each time she remembered it. She felt, each time, the school bus seat sticking to her sweaty derrière; she saw Russell boarding, climbing the steps with his empty backpack, finding her three rows back, in the seat they always shared. "My head hurts," he'd told her, as he slid beside her into sitting. "It hurts real bad." The only thing that changed, in Ruth's reliving it, was that each time, she felt even more scorched with regret at having said nothing to her brother then, not having hugged him or touched his head: it had seemed to her, then, not like a medical emergency but like a regular moment on the school bus, anathemic to public displays of familial affection.

By the time the bus turned into their neighborhood, Russell was crying. "I want to lick the cold, cold floor," he told their mother, when he cleared the front door. Ruth's mother gave him an aspirin and sent him to bed, but not even an hour later, Wendy passed by his room and heard him taking shallow, desperate breaths. "For the love of God," she screamed downstairs, "can't you hear him? One of you people needs to call a fucking ambulance."

The ambulance carried Russell away as it would carry any innocent, sickly child during the Lenten season, but when Ruth's mother climbed in the back door and told them to call their father, Ruth heard some new air of finality in her voice. The EMT had closed the door on the scene of her mother leaning over Russell; Ruth heard the sound of the latch as it shut, the wrong emptiness of her mother's not mentioning when she'd return. She hadn't mentioned, either, Ruth and Wendy's joining them at the hospital later. Ruth's mother had run upstairs after Wendy screamed, she'd touched Russell there in his bed, and must have instantly known.

Though she couldn't possibly have known the details, how surgeons would repair Russell's ruptured aorta in a nine-hour surgery that would, after insurance, bankrupt them; that post-surgery, he'd linger on in the hospital for thirty-nine of the longest hours Ruth could ever have imagined, opening his eyes every so often to register them all as they hid behind one another, speaking what they hoped were soothing words. Ruth wasn't certain that the words were good ones. And she hadn't been confident that Russell was even actually looking at them, because his eyes had been composed of little other than sheer terror.

"He's at peace," her mother said that Wednesday, when she had the school office call Ruth out of her French class to speak on the telephone. But Ruth knew he wasn't. And even at the funeral, as they lowered her little brother's casket down into upper Earth, Ruth felt that if it suddenly fell open, what she'd be looking at was the terror in her brother's wide-set eyes.

Wendy came and got Ruth at school. Wendy was a new driver, with just a permit, and in retrospect, Ruth would pin the rootless grief down to Wendy's behind-the-wheel nerves, but they drove to the hospital without crying, without talking, without even the emptiness of talk radio as cognitive dissonance. Ruth couldn't have known that she was losing Wendy too, that the sister who'd played chess with her, and written misspelled love notes to her in kindergarten, dragged her around their room by one arm when she was a baby, was now going to absorb this tragedy completely and leave them all. Ruth remembered that, when they got to the hospital that day, her father's old blue Nissan was still parked in the hospital's entrance circle, its windows rolled halfway down on both sides.

"Wow. I can't believe they haven't towed dad's car," Wendy said.

Ruth supposed, silently, that someone had notified the front desk that the sad, old car belonged to the dead kid's father. The dead kid's family, Ruth knew they'd be known as now at the hospital. The dead kid's sister, people at school would call her. The dead kid's dad. The dead kid's mom. The dead kid's grandpa. The dead kid.

She decided rather quickly that she wouldn't let Russell's death hem her in as any one thing or another, and going forward, moving on to new situations in life, she told no one. In the Public Cosmology of Ruth she was no longer the middle child, but the younger of two girls. No, there hadn't been any boys in her family, she'd tell people, and at times she'd even unravel the half-truth that sure, her parents had always wanted a son. By the time she met James, both her parents had passed on—young, in their fifties, still full of shame and grief—and Wendy was speaking to her on order of twice a year, so it had been easy to simply omit the information permanently. She erased it so cleanly from the part of her mind that accessed language that Russell became present only as a figure of deepest cellular memory, and she'd almost forgotten about his death in a conscious way until she became pregnant with Annie, and then what had come to her was that none of this had been her parents' fault. All those years they'd blamed themselves for a simple trick of genetics, for what she and Wendy found out later, after science began to reveal all the new diseases, was a simple missing chromosomal period. A tiny hiccup of nature that had cost her family everything.

But only in her first trimester had she let the thoughts in, and for most of her adult life, in the most real, daily part of her mind, only small hurtful things came to her now and then, jogged by certain colors she saw in the supermarket, or certain situations she spied between families in the street. Like this tattooed teenage girl they see leaning against a car now as Clarisse drives past her, how the girl summons Ruth's memory of Wendy's worldweary lope as she walked over to their father's car there in the hospital circle the day Russell died. The defiance in her gait had already solidified into something more adult, more codified, something that knew everything it needed to know about the unfairness of the world. But Ruth doesn't remember what happened next, whether Wendy moved the car. Ruth doesn't remember how Wendy would have had their father's keys. So the memory goes blank in her mind like the end of a television programming day. Fizz. Fuzz.

Which is the way it works after she and Clarisse have walked in the cold to a Mexican restaurant not far down Bardstown Road, after they've trotted next door to a bar for whisky sours, after she's had a second whisky sour to Clarisse's third and then sat on her stool laughing with Clarisse in order to "sober up," after Clarisse has driven her back to her car and told her she's going to wait there until she's sure Ruth gets in her car okay.

Ruth starts her car and waves at Clarisse in her rearview mirror, then waits for her friend to back up and pull out of the parking lot before she herself proceeds: she drives the five miles to James' house, her old house: she puts the key in the back door lock that James will never hear—he's such a sound sleeper and it's far from his upstairs bedroom—and she turns it softly, and then sighs with relief that he hasn't yet changed the locks. She thinks of the hideous amaryllis James brought home for her birthday, how it would have to have been after he changed his computer password.

And that's the last thing she thinks.

She doesn't think of anything at all, in fact, until she gets his frantic call, at 3:30 in the morning. "It's Annie," he says, the words gushing out so fast their ends touch. "The house. There was a fire."

"ABSOLUTELY NOT," Ruth's mother said, without conviction.

No one else stood at the top of the stairs, where she and Ruth had met accidentally on their way between floors, but she wasn't talking to Ruth. She was just saying it, as she did on order of thirty times a week now that Russell was dead.

"Absolutely not," she'd say in response to nothing, as she was folding laundry, or stacking china, or scrubbing tomato paste out of the sink. The first few times, she caught herself and blinked, and Ruth could tell that she'd been taken aback by the machinations of her own mind—she hadn't meant to issue the two words audibly.

But her mother soon lost shame. She started saying it seemingly at random, producing the phrase from some secret, outraged vein of thought. "Absolutely not," she said one morning at dawn, in the kitchen, where Ruth had gone looking for food. When her mother heard her, she turned around, and her posture seemed confrontational, as though she were hiding something. But when Ruth got closer and looked, it was just the percolating machine on the counter behind her. Her mother turned back around. "Absolutely not," she whispered to the coffee, and Ruth forgot what she needed from the refrigerator and went back to bed.

When her mother said it in response to an actual question, after Wendy asked if she could have a brand new stereo system for Christmas, Ruth started crying. "Absolutely not," her mother said then, in response to her tears, and Ruth bolted upstairs to her bedroom.

She no longer shared her bedroom with Russell but she shared it with the aftermath of Russell, his swim participation trophies and the lopsided clay masks he'd made in the third grade, his fourth and last year of formal schooling. No one had even changed his bedsheets—they'd lain, hastily rolled to one side, for the three days after his death, until finally, the morning of his funeral, her mother had come into the room and made his bed up to hotel standards. When Ruth came home from the funeral and tossed a quarter at the sheets, it actually bounced once before landing.

It took a week for Ruth to grow tired of seeing the stiff bed, so empty of her brother, and she sat on it then, hard, hoping to leave an impression of her own living, breathing ass. She lay on his pillow and rolled onto her face. She left rumpling, dimpling. She began to reassemble his things into piles: plastic cowboy collection in the northeast corner of the room, Spider Man comic books in the southwest corner, near the head of her own bed. The room wasn't his anymore, but it was no longer hers, either. Now that he was dead it was just a room, four walls a floor a ceiling and an exactly square window hurtling with her around the center of the planet through different points of time; since no one but her entered the room now, she'd been left as some sort of gatekeeper, contemplating the limitations of the human references the room still contained. The things left in the room weren't shrine to her dead brother so much as they were now shrine to impossibility, and the failed hope for all the things Russell had so rarely touched when he was alive. She felt vicious, scooting aside his Lego cabin with the edge of her bare foot, but she persisted in pushing it to the wall, even as it fell in half and then crumbled into chunks of joined plastic bricks.

She arranged all his socks and all his clothes, first by color, and then by size, into assorted piles. Over time, she discarded and rearranged his effects until she'd assembled several assorted piles of Russell, which someone came and cleared one day while she was at school. She opened the door to find it all gone and she gasped, audibly— the mess itself had become as a living, breathing human, so that when it was gone, she missed it. She came home two days later to find Russell's bed and nightstand similarly disappeared. She didn't dare ask what had happened. She wouldn't have called herself relieved. She hadn't wanted to clear her brother from her life. She'd simply wanted to proceed with her own.

Her parents were still paying hospital bills for a dead child. The financial difficulty showed up incrementally: her mother's "absolutely not" when Ruth asked whether they could go on a vacation that summer, her father's uncharacteristic purchase of a lottery ticket, which she found hidden in his office drawer when she went looking for a sharpened pencil. It took six months for her mother to tell them that eating off paper plates was cheaper than running the drawer when she went looking for a sharpened pencil. It took six months for her mother to tell them that eating off paper plates was cheaper than running the dishwasher, and another four for her mother to run out of money at the supermarket.

Ruth had been helping unload provisions from the cart when she noticed the man behind them, who had joined the line after they started unloading. The man seemed to be appraising her, and she felt embarrassed to be unloading such an intimate item as supermarket brand toilet paper. He took a few steps back to scan the other check-outs for a shorter wait time but, seeing nothing, remained in line behind them: as Ruth removed the 28 ounces of canned peas (which, in the new family economy, replaced the sixteen ounces of frozen), the man shifted impatiently from foot to foot. Ruth tried not to glare. He seemed to know nothing about the patience that grief demanded of people.

"$64.39," the clerk told her mother, after he'd punched the last of their order into his register.

Ruth saw her mother's shoulders slacken. Her mother counted and then recounted the three twenties in her hand as though another one might magically appear. She took her purse off her shoulder and dug through its depths. Ruth could see the new gray hair at her temples glistening in the supermarket's fluorescent lights.

"Put back the eggs," she told Ruth.

Ruth took the eggs and prepared to walk to the dairy in the rear of the store, but before she could get around him, the man behind her was handing her mother a five-dollar bill. "Please," he said. His voice was kind, but Ruth was afraid. She was afraid that her mother was going to take money from this impatient white man. It was so critical that she didn't.

"Absolutely not," her mother said, but with such little conviction that the man handed his five past her shoulder to the cashier. Her mother turned meekly towards him and said "Thank you. Thank you so much." To Ruth, it sounded as an earthquake. She knew that her mother had lost, in that moment, the small amount of power she'd had left in the world.

WHATEVER ANNIE HAS going on now in the hospital isn't at all serious. It's not going to kill Annie and it's not going to bankrupt Ruth or James. But the accident has tapped Ruth on the shoulder and notified her that the danger is never over, that death will be hovering in a corner, grinning and whispering, so long as her child is still alive. Annie's left arm is bandaged from shoulder to wrist and she's knocked out with heavy pain medication, and Ruth is stroking the hand on the arm that isn't burned, marveling at how smooth it is, still just a child's hand, no matter how many times Annie uses it to text the word *shit* to her friends on Instagram.

There's a tray of food that's been wheeled in by a different, younger nurse, with a bowl of tomato soup and a piece of desiccated yellow cornbread that Annie will never eat. When Annie wakes, Ruth plans to feed her the soup, spoon it into her mouth like she's a little bird, because Annie is left-handed but it's her left arm that must stay stationary and elevated to prevent fluid buildup.

It's just, thank God, a second degree burn. In a month, the doctor told them, after the blisters have sunk back into lymph, and the arm's coloring returned to some semblance of its olive color, it will seem as though the burn never happened. Still, James disappeared a few minutes after Annie fell asleep, perhaps because he could no longer sit across Annie's bed and look Ruth in the eye. This house fire that almost killed his daughter happened in his no-longer-hers house, on his now-completely-his weekend custody watch.

"Oh dear God Ruth I'm so sorry," he'd said in a rush, when she arrived at the hospital. Ruth had never heard him cry before, and she went queasy when she saw what an ugly crier he was. He sounded like a goose. One up for slaughter. It was such ugly crying, with his eyelids turned red and snot glistening in the caves of his nostrils, that she almost told him none of this was his fault, that it wasn't like he was a pyromaniac or an arsonist. That it was an authentic accident such as could happen to any parent.

But she wouldn't say that out loud. She wouldn't tell him it was okay, or he was fine, or everything was going to be all right. This was the bargain of getting divorced—forgiveness was no longer an allowable feeling. There were lawyers now, and temporary orders, and document production—there was no profit whatsoever in mercy. When at last James broke his sobs, she put the steel in her voice to ask how it happened.

He leveled his eyes with hers, and then rose and went to the window, where he put his forehead against the glass. She imagined the glass was cool against his head, but the sun was screaming as it sank, setting the edges of his silhouette ablaze. "Fire started in the basement," he said. "In the trash can near the sink."

"How can they pinpoint it that precisely?"

James shrugged. "That's their job. I'm sure it's a science."

"Well, what was in it?" Ruth asked, though she already knew.

"Unidentifiable organic materials. And a flowerpot. Which is so weird. I didn't put it there and Annie denies it. No idea how it got there."

Ruth knew. For three tenths of a second, she definitely knew. But then, at the four tenths mark, she didn't. "Weird," she said. Honestly.

They'd driven down to Mammoth Cave once when Annie was little, right after she lost her first tooth, and Annie had insisted on going to one of the little bungalow tourist shops, where she made Ruth buy her small rocks glued to labelled cards. *Igneous*, read her favorite, a card affixed with a black, five-centimeter rock in the shape of a teardrop. Ruth wrapped it in tissue paper and put it in a Ziploc bag so that Annie could take it to school for show and tell. *That rock you're holding?* she remembered telling Annie. *It was liquid when it came out of the middle of the earth. Like raspberry filling from a Valentine's chocolate, but so hot you couldn't have held it or even gotten near it. If you'd held it then, when it first came out of the earth, it would have melted your hand down through the flesh and into the bone.* Whatever someone had thrown in the trash, Ruth thought, blinking, forgetting, knowing but not understanding how, then not knowing at all. It had killed her house. Endangered her child.

"Oh," she said now to James. "Shit. Will insurance still pay?"

"Yeah I guess. I mean, it was still an accident."

"Well," she said.

James turned and walked back to her, planted his toes so that his face was suddenly inches from hers, right in her personal space. She couldn't move because she wouldn't move. She had the obscene urge to kiss him. It could be like he'd just dropped her home after a date. She quickly recognized the urge as belonging less to anything that had happened between them and more to banal, human, physical default.

"And the structure?" Ruth asked. "I mean, is *anything* left?"

James started crying again, in soft honks, and it took several stops and starts of his voice for him to tell her. "There's a whole crew there now. Chopping into the walls to check for leftover embers. Ripping up the carpets," he said, his voice going high in his Adam's apple to stanch a new break into weeping. Ruth couldn't bear to hear him cry again, so she dropped her questioning. She accepted silence, his blessed silence.

Annie had been awake, but only in the vaguest way, when he started talking: now, Ruth saw her eyelids flicker, and she lost herself to sleep, felled under the weight of the Demerol. James was watching Annie too, she guessed, over her shoulder, and he'd moved close enough behind Ruth that she could smell the soot in his hair. The Red Cross had given him a change of clothes, but he had yet to shower. He'd been at the hospital with Annie through the night.

"I left the door open when I ran out," he said, "but apparently that was the dumbest thing I could have done."

"Because?"

"Fire sucks oxygen through an open door. Just like a vacuum cleaner."

As he spoke, the nurse who'd brought the Demerol came in to check Annie's monitor, and when she saw James standing so close, she gave Ruth a smile that Ruth interpreted as heartwarmed: she'd misinterpreted James' physical proximity as intimacy. Ruth determined, then, to hate the nurse, with her large round eyes and perfect fish lips. This was maybe also the balance of a divorce, she thought, that you had to hate everyone who wasn't cheering you on in it.

James continued, telling her how the fire had fed itself through the door and kicked into higher gear once they were outside. "And then the roof fell in. Or I shouldn't say 'fell,' because that's not what it did. The house just sucked its own roof right down its throat. I pulled Annie across the street, but I accidentally took her burned arm, so she screamed. And it wasn't like it is in the movies, Ruth. It took me so long after the roof crashed in, to grab Annie. And then it was like I had to *remember* to run. That was the worst part, thinking that if we'd been standing any closer, we might have died."

He was a good enough storyteller that Ruth felt bedraggled, as though she'd been there with him, enduring the danger. She angled her head to look up at him and make one slow, pronounced bat of her eyelashes that she hoped came across as nastiness. *You'll never have Annie on the weekend again*, she knew the balance of divorce required her to say. *You almost killed my child. I'll petition the court for sole custody. Don't think I won't.* It wasn't what she felt, though, so she said something only a fraction as hurtful. "Well," she sighed. "Listen. After all that? I don't see you spooning food carefully down a burn victim's throat. Why don't you make yourself useful? Press the call button over there and ask the nurse for more—"

But instead, he left. And when she got up and looked after him, down the hall to the nurse's station, he wasn't there. He understood too, then, that a proper divorce required continual bad will.

He came back an hour later wearing the same donated clothes, still smelling like a chimneysweep, his eyes as wild as she'd ever seen them. She asked him nothing. In their respective positions across the room—she in the hardback chair next to Annie's bed and he on the blue leather couch the hospital had put in the room to invite coziness—they watched television through the evening. "We've got to tell Annie," he said, in the middle of Anderson Cooper 360. "Everything's gone. Her whole life, just gone."

"She'll live. I mean, that's the important thing, is that we made it out of the house."

They both slept another night in Annie's room, she in bed alongside Annie's good arm, and he on the sofa, sprawled in such a way that he now looked like he was growing out of the blue leather, like the sofa was some kind of James planter. Early the next morning, the fish-lipped nurse came to change Annie's bandages.

"You're still on shift?" Ruth asked.

"I'm working a double. Trying to pay off my car."

The nurse unwrapped and rewrapped so quickly that Ruth couldn't imagine she'd noted or examined anything, but when she was finished she said, "Looks good. Healing up well," and Ruth blacked the earlier hatred out of her mind.

"Good luck," she said, as the nurse gathered her things and rushed out of the room.

A different nurse returned with a cup of orange juice, and Ruth held it at the level of Annie's chin so she could suck out of the bent plastic straw without moving her arm.

"Dad," Annie said. She was wide awake. "Go. Take a shower or something. Sleep. Mom's got this. Go."

James' eyes turned red, and Ruth feared he'd start his ugly crying anew, but instead he said, quietly, "I think I'm going to check into a Holiday Inn." Ruth was grateful, so grateful. She was tired of smelling his soot.

Moreover, because her emotions were primarily resentful ones, she knew she had to be the one to tell Annie that all was lost. She'd be able to say it without emotion, in a way James wouldn't, not for years. She'd tell Annie that—guess what—she didn't have to put away her laundry when she got home because now she had no laundry.

She had no clothes at all, save the ones she'd left at Ruth's apartment. She had none of the frilly, polyester-blend dresses Ruth had boxed up and saved from Easters past, as though Annie might suddenly shrink to size and relive them. She had none of the toddler toys Ruth hadn't been able to bear discarding or taking to Goodwill—the fire had solved the problem of sentimentality. She'd explain to Annie that the past was now free and clear; that she had no ribbons from the gymnastics team she'd quit in a meet-inspired rage at age ten; no pink down comforter, a gift from her Grandma Pauline that was starting to fray at its edges. No favorite young adult novels to reread over the summer, no Wallace and Gromit DVD's to remind her of a time before hormones. Everything that hadn't burned or melted had been drowned in sheets of water, courtesy the Middletown Fire Protection District's engine #2. *It's okay*, Ruth planned on saying. *You shouldn't need material things to know who you were, or who you are now. We'll get you another cell phone, and insurance will replace the iPad. My dear, the earth is still spinning under your feet.*

But Ruth knew, because she'd lived a version of it herself, that this child was going to have a mighty job picking up the pieces of her life. With a burned dominant arm. Between her parents' houses, with their differing bedtimes, their varying rules. Annie was, at age thirteen, going to have to learn to be ambidextrous.

Ruth remembered. She remembered forgetting Russell. She remembered the process she used to forget his smell, the way she told herself aloud that the smell belonged to other things, even as she sorted and rearranged the clothes and toys and artworks that were undeniably Russell's. *It's peanut butter*, she would say, when it came to her on the stale air of her room. *It's Tide*. She remembered how, even after someone came and removed all Russell's clothes, his smell lingered in the closet, a smell of saltines and new grass and boyhood, molecules of things that had touched the living Russell, and she told herself that it was just drifting through her open window. She remembered how in late summer, when the temperature rose and he seemed to be everywhere in the room with her, she'd repeat to herself over and over again that on some level, it meant he'd never been anywhere.

She remembered forgetting. And if she let herself, she started to remember how, two nights ago, she'd keyed into James' house and quite possibly accidentally started the fire that almost killed Annie. But then she pushed the memory down before it could emerge even half-formed. She hadn't. Done anything. She hadn't been there at all. If asked during an investigation, she would just forget to remember. Because here's what she'd learned herself, at Annie's age: remembering could kill you.

STUART FRIEBERT

Sorry, I Don't

1

IN THE '60S, DAVID YOUNG and I received an Oberlin College grant—to foster faculty development in ancillary interests—that enabled us to visit a number of German poets in hopes of putting together a textbook/anthology, which would present a selection of their poems, followed by a series of questions we put to them, and ending with their responses. Some colleagues, knowing full well that we were just beginning to make a mark with our own poems and translations, wondered, as indeed we also did, whether or not the likes of Günter Eich and his mate Ilse Aichinger, Günter Grass, Paul Celan, Karl Krolow, Hilde Domin, Helmut Heißenbüttel, and Rainer Brambach, all well on their way to illustrious careers, would open the door for relative unknowns. But open the door they all did, which alas did not result in our ever completing said textbook, but did begin lifelong relationships and result in many translations they allowed us to publish through the years.

Having been one of the first exchange students to study in Germany after WW II (1949-50), originally sent to study science and mathematics, I had become swept up in linguistic issues while studying with Prof. Karl Langosch, the great medievalist, which upon return led me to a PhD in German, and many years of teaching the language and literature. It was a complex time in Germany—about which I've written two memoirs[1]—and that year's experiences have preoccupied me ever since, further complicated by being Jewish, having lost many relatives at the hands of the Nazis— and THEN having met Paul Celan, which finally emboldened me to write poems and prose in German.[2]

But back to Berlin, Grass' sort-of brownstone at Niedstraße 14, if memory of the exact address holds. We'd come from productive visits with all the others, and would fly on to Paris for our final meeting with Celan, the memory of which, by the by, still haunts to this day (as I've also referenced elsewhere). Having been advised by a colleague to stay at the Hotel Continental in Berlin, he did not mention that the

---

[1] *The Language of the Enemy (Black Mountain Press); First & Last Words (Pinyon Publishing).*
[2] *Kein Trinkwasser (poems; Atelier Verlag); Die Prokuristen kommen (poems; Lenos Presse); Der Gast, und sei er noch so schlecht (prose sketches; Gilles & Francke Verlag); Nicht hinauslehnen (poems; Delp Verlag).*

overflowing bowl of fruit awaiting us in our room was not a welcoming present and would add more than $200 by the time we checked out, inasmuch as we somehow overlooked a little list of the cost of each piece of fruit. My wife still sort of jokes when she says she had to pawn the wedding silverware when I wired for an extra $200 we'd not budgeted.

We slept the first night rather fitfully, excited at the prospect of attending Brecht's *Threepenny Opera* at the Berliner Ensemble Theater in East Berlin the next day, which Helene Weigel had invited us to after we'd written her about hoping to include some of Bert Brecht's poems in our anthology, adding she might be able to answer some questions about them. Thanks to her invitation on official stationery of the Berliner Ensemble, transiting Checkpoint Charlie to enter the East Zone was a breeze. Alas, when we arrived at the box office, she sent a note down that she was indisposed, but hoped we'd enjoy the performance from her personal box. David and I revisit this occasion during our bimonthly lunches, among a host of other shared experiences over the course of a special friendship that's lasted since we were both hired at Oberlin in 1961.

Having written to each writer in advance with an offer to bring anything "special" they might prize as a gift, we heard from Grass on the usual postcard he communicated with that he'd not mind having some decent if not Cuban cigars—at the time I believe there were certain embargoes in effect—and his cognac supply was running low. (A postcard-aside: when I sent him one of my early German poems about bombing raids over Germany, his postcard shot back with a poem about his jets shooting down my bombers.) So off course we scoured Berlin for the best cigars and cognac we could buy, which required some justifying when we presented our receipts to Oberlin's comptroller upon return.

Preceding him when he opened the door, that bushy mustache! Steel-rimmed glasses reminded of Brecht's. Slightly hunched, if he straightened up he'd top our heights. A no-nonsense look about him, not one to shake your hand lightly, he then gestured, bowing slightly, toward a staircase after securing our gift package under an arm. Up we climbed, huffing and puffing by the time we reached what might have been the third or fourth floor and were shown into something of a gymnasium, with a basketball hoop at one end and ample space for the gang of kids running about, now busy skirmishing over a soccer ball, now shooting a basketball at the hoop. At the other end, a little spiral staircase, if memory serves, led up to an elevated platform overlooking the playing field below. "My eagle's nest," I think he said and allowed as how he liked writing up there to the background music of the neighbor kids playing with Grass' below.

"Let's have one of your cigars before we find out exactly why you're here," he said and, noticing the cognac, "something of a chaser." Opening a drawer in the desk, he parked nifty little shot glasses before us. We took out copies of his poems we wanted to include, but before spelling out the nature of the project, mentioning the other poets also aboard, I took a moment to warm up the atmosphere by way of letting Grass know his work in general was being taught by a number of us in Oberlin's German Department; and recounted that only recently, during a discussion of his novella *Cat and Mouse* in my Conversation & Composition class, there was a knock at the door. I shouted, and a man quickly entered, austere looking, albeit nattily dressed, likely a European I told myself judging from his look, his haircut. I pointed to a seat in the back and he waved, then put his finger to his lips as if to say he'd be quiet, which got the whole class smiling. It wasn't parents' weekend, but on occasion parents would ask to sit in on a class; and we quickly returned to the text. After the class filed out at session's end, the man approached me rather stiffly, bowed his head slightly and, I underlined for Grass, softly clicked his heels together; reminiscent of actors portraying German officials or military, I couldn't help sensing. To this day I can hear the man saying his name—Wernher von Braun—and the few words of thanks he offered in crisp German, ending on "quite interesting." Not until he left did I realize Iris von Braun, a student in class, was his daughter. That calls for another shot of cognac, Grass said and proposed a toast something along the lines of *c'est la vie!*

After he approved the list of poems we wanted to include, we asked some questions on two accounts: ours, to make sure we basically understood the poems; and slightly less complex ones we felt would make students more comfortable taking them on. Aside, as I recall, from teasing us about applying a double standard, stopping painfully short of accusing us of dumbing them down, he startled us by insisting nothing in the texts could not be tracked down; in encyclopedias, library archives, even public records and almanacs—by the by as Celan also did, in spades, when we referenced many more instances in his poems where we had no clue, a not uncommon feeling among otherwise sophisticated readers of his poems.

Our time was up, but before Grass showed us out he suggested—if we were interested and had time (I think we'd have rebooked a flight if we had to!)—we might join him at a rehearsal of his new play, *The Plebeians Rehearse the Uprising* at the Schiller Theater the next day. We found him hunkered down in one of the back rows of the darkened auditorium and slipped into a row behind. During the hour or so we decided it was polite and prudent to stay, he might have whispered an occasional remark over his shoulder as he scribbled away at a clipboard, but all I recall is a single sentence that has stuck to this day: "No one has the courage to tell me what isn't working." Whispering our great thanks, we crept out. A few weeks after our return to Oberlin, David recalls getting a book of Grass' poems he'd inscribed in a tiny script, "Vielen Dank für die europäischen Zigarren!" which we donated to the library's Special Collections. David has since opined that Grass hoped the play would establish him as more than worthy of assuming Brecht's mantle, given Grass' support of revolting workers, whereas Brecht chose to remain silent during the uprising in East Germany in June, 1953, when threats of Soviet intervention restored "order." At the time, to add insult to the workers' pleas for help from Brecht and others of his station and stature, Brecht was adapting Shakespeare's *Coriolanus* with his Berliner Ensemble compatriots. (The finished version would not be staged till 1962.)

2

IN THE '90s, when I was working with Karl Krolow on a volume of his selected poems and staying in a small inn southeast of Darmstadt, I hiked over to Reichelsheim, where Krolow recommended I could enjoy a "respectable lunch; and be sure to match it to a local wine." After needing several espressos to stay awake after the repast, I strolled around the picturesque town before heading back to my digs, mindful I'd promised the elderly innkeeper to exercise his chow chow. Just before it was time to hurry back, my eye caught sight of a poster in the city hall's window, advertising a reading, the very next day, by Günter Grass in the hall's auditorium! Hopeful Krolow would understand my request to postpone our get-together for another day—which he was happy to do provided I'd deliver a review—I knew I'd have an early hike back in the morning to have a chance at getting a seat for the noon reading, as I recall the announcement read. Dimly aware that Grass had just published a new novel, which a number of critics found wanting—even local papers took notice—I'd also heard from a friend in Berlin that Grass was thinking of sticking it to them by going on a reading tour of much smaller venues, defiantly not large cities he was accustomed to tour; but, my friend said, small towns and even villages of his "real readers."

Though I arrived an hour early for the reading, it seemed clear from the throng already lining the hallway inside city hall and spooling out into the street, waiting for the doors to the chamber to open, that I stood little chance of getting in, much less finding a seat. Nonetheless, I did what others were doing, this not being the U.K. and queuing not even a lost art, and wedged into the crowd. Minutes later someone announced with a megaphone that though the doors would soon open, we were to remain in place, as Herr Grass and his entourage would be arriving any moment to take their seats on the stage. We turned back to the street and there he was, exiting a car. His frame I recalled from thirty years or so ago had perhaps filled out some, but nothing else seemed different as he approached, save perhaps for graying hair and, more notably, heavily-lidded eyes. A moment after he passed the clump I stood in, he suddenly stopped when the man with the megaphone reached him and whispered something. Now turned toward the chamber whose doors were wide open, we could see a long table on the stage. The next thing I knew Grass himself began tapping a few of us on the shoulder, upon which we were quickly hustled along after him by his staff and directed toward the table. Later we learned Grass was eager to see as many of us seated as possible, no matter where! After Grass took his seat, stage center, the man who'd introduce him—perhaps the mayor?—sat down immediately to his right, and next to him, as instructed, "me, myself, and I." My brain couldn't stop chattering. It did occur to me while the introduction droned on that Grass had perhaps singled me out because he recognized me somehow from our visit long ago . . .

Not having come with the new novel for him to autograph, nor having read so much as a line, I listened half distracted. Like Grass and all of us at the table, I was looking out at the audience seated in something of a bowl the chamber's shape assumed, and my eyes began swimming. I do recall Grass reading clearly but softly, like a good actor not melodramatically, which some of the more humorous passages might have invited. When he turned the last page of the chapter he read from, pushing back to stretch out, carefully taking his glasses off, there was at first a hushed silence before someone began to clap methodically, one clap following another slowly, eventually building to a crescendo the crowd joined in more and more forcefully. If I'd stood to signal a standing O, as I might have back home, I'd have remained the only soul to do so. Finally, with a light wave, Grass brought the applause to a halt, and someone announced a line could form for those with the novel to sign. For a moment I thought I might just lean over, say my thanks, perhaps reference our visit back when. That quickly became impossible, as the rest of us were hurried off the stage, so I decided to wait in line for a word, which took some maneuvering. Once again, queuing was on no one's mind; just scrambling, sometimes in groups of three or four, was clearly the rule.

Moving along slowly, I tried to rehearse a few lines after adding my thanks for a moving reading, which in some ways it had been though I was partly adrift: the whole room had reverberated with reverence it would have been hard to escape. The closer I got to Grass, the more nervous I grew, sensing my voice dwindling.

When I was next, I felt weak and put both palms to the table, trying not to lean too close. He'd been looking down, fumbling with his pen. When he looked up, I felt him looking through me to the next woman in line. Something kicked in and I blurted out "Niedstrasse 14! Where my colleague and I visited you in Berlin, wonder if you remember?"—foolishly hoping that, by mentioning his actual address, he would remember. But then what? He seemed to look at the woman behind, over my shoulder, as if to say, what's with this guy? My last words tumbled out, "Surely you remember the cigars and cognac?!"—which to this moment makes me cringe.

His last words to me were, "Sorry, I don't . . ." All Krolow did when I recounted the tale was pat me on the hand, which was still trembling.

ALL that was some years before Grass' long-kept "secret" was finally revealed, which he spent many of his years left trying to address—he famously said, "It was a weight on me"; not only to rebut his fiercest critics, some of whom, even now that he's gone, remain convinced his intent all along was to "cover up," fudge details, downright dissemble. What we know for sure when he was "outed" is that he had indeed joined the Hitlerjugend (at age 10!), as was almost de rigeuer. Barely seventeen, Grass was eventually drafted into the "Waffen SS," Heinrich Himmler's brainchild, the armed wing of the Nazi Party's SS organization, ultimately condemned at Nuremberg for its criminal acts. At that age, like so many young souls, he was easily caught up in the grandeur and pomp, in my view. Some of his detractors claim he did so with excessive fervor and pride, noting he volunteered for submarine duty, a command that enjoyed great popularity and respect among the populace. However, he was instead assigned to a tank unit and eventually captured in that command. For a moving and I believe faithful account of those years, his essay, "How I Spent the War," which appeared in the June 4th, 2007 issue of *The New Yorker*, is essential reading.

Yellowing notes have recently brought me back to that unnerving day in the '60s when I was teaching Grass' superb novella, *Cat and Mouse*, recounted to Grass. Caught up in the thrall of the novella's plot, easily identifying with the young protagonists, who dive down to explore a sunken Polish sub among other adventures, and in which an Iron Cross figures powerfully, my students always got round to wondering how they might have responded, behaved, in those fearful circumstances. However, back then, it never occurred to any of us, as it finally does now, that Grass was making his tortured way through his own submerged ruins, as he surely was throughout all the work. How I'd want him to know Adrienne Rich's "Diving into the Wreck"! Unless of course he did . . .

ERIKA JO BROWN

Mary Ruefle Poem

Mary Ruefle advised me to stand underneath the weeping
Alaskan spruce—it was actually a cedar—and so I did
for a few minutes, enough to narrate the thought
that Mary Ruefle told me to stand underneath a tree.
Then I went for a walk by the lake. Restless and skeptical,
perceive, perceive, I commanded myself. I saw a teen
writing in his journal, and jealousy rippled through me,
for his focus and dumb face and all he doesn't know
is coming after him. Consciousness is the brain turning
on itself. I regret not bringing bug spray is one of those
fuddy-duddy distractions, or how silly to wear sandals
down here. Those thoughts doublestuff themselves
into my mind's eye socket. Fire ants and spiders and unknown
animals shuffling among the ferns. We're aware of consequence,
sequence, cause and effect, we all know how this ends.

JUAN MORALES

Secret Maintenance

Home became a tangle of curtains, picture frames, and a flipped-over welcome mat.

Home became furniture and linens I didn't use enough,

but still protected with a vacuum, rags, and cleaners.

The house became a monument to screwdrivers, hammers, brushes, and pliers

where I once had thought I'd die happy.

Somewhere between the ticks of lonely clocks ceasing, me and my minus one.

I became caretaker for the creaks of the house still settling,

maintenance that secretly devastated me.

MOLLY SPENCER

Disclosures | If You Are Aware of Any Nuisance Animals Such as Crows, Chickens, or Barking Dogs

The crows will go on gathering
inside you. The crows will repeat
and repeat their hooked questions—

> *when in the interior*
> *who amidst the birches*
> *why   why   deadfall   why*

The crows will creak and rasp like hinges. You'll wake to
days that stain your hands, bits of char

from a beach-fire, some forgotten summer. Days
that, like the crows, want answers—

> *if in the understory*
> *where the front crosses over the sky above you*
> *if you have untied your heart from the blood-knot*
> > *and left the strings loose*
> > > *and desultory*   *now what*

The crows will follow you home wanting to know

> *are you happy now are you   happy*

Now that you've lost your faith in the slope
of the roof. Now that it's snowing
again and the whole world pretends

to soften. The crows will preside over your quiet
ritual of diminishment, calling out
sharp threats.

      if by rafter   you mean rib

If the moan of a northing train
is what's left to listen to. If it's a different train now
but just as forlorn.

Now that the only scrape of a shovel over the walk before daylight
is your scrape.

Now that the blade in your hands is the blade that you asked for.

ARTHUR RUSSELL

Burning Garbage

I

My father considered it a kind of birthright to burn garbage,
as long as he did it skillfully. Skill was his morality,

and burning garbage fit his basic rule of business:
at the end of the day, we must go home with all of the money.

That was Brooklyn, washing cars for the summer, and at 26,
or precisely whatever age I was, and my dad, at 66, we were strong,

and I had another year on my creative writing fellowship at Syracuse,
looking towards the Spring of '84 for a free write.

Fear of falling back into my father's orbit made me prickly,
but I was anyway at the height of a certain set of abilities:

I could count money, fix machines, wire appliances,
stand in the street with a damp towel on my shoulder,

supervise men, hand out tickets, vacuum cars, steam mats,
scrub white walls, dry bumpers, wipe windows, change motors, go to the bank,

reach between the dripping brushes in the path of cars
on the conveyor line, and collect fallen license plates,

or catch up and jump into a moving car that slipped into gear
and was bouncing down the track, yank open the door and jam my foot on the brake.

I could go up on the roof on a summer day with Prince McMichael,
smoke cigarettes and slosh tar with a spent broom on the roof seams,

and listen to him talk in disrespectful terms about the women he had known,
take the stitches out of Pete Watson's head with a tweezer and razor blade

so he wouldn't have to take time off to go to the doctor,
or I could follow Sam Tyler when he left his post and ambled toward the deli,

to stop him from buying beer,
and I could burn garbage smokelessly in the yard behind our building.

II

We burned garbage in a 55-gallon barrel that John Casey prepared by removing
the top with a barrel-sized can opener and hammering the jagged edges flat.

Then he stove holes in the barrel sides with a pick ax,
and set it on a pair of I-beams with a milk crate inside.

One of those barrels would last about a year
before the steel collapsed like foil, disintegrated to rust in the fire and the rain.

Casey was a big-boned, white-haired, rosy-checked, mostly toothless
Irishman of the old school, and another time I'll tell you

how he wasted his astonishing big-boned youth, and lost his wife
and nearly died of alcohol in that self-same car-wash yard, until he saved himself.

For now, I'll say he collected the garbage from the trash cans with a hand truck—
newspapers mostly, coffee cups, whatever—wet it down with gasoline, and lit it.

On a good day, with a good fire, the garbage burned so hot and fast
the people whose houses backed up to the car wash yard would see no smoke.

The flames would seem no more than the heat waves surrounding Omar Sharif
as he approached from a great distance in *Lawrence of Arabia*.

But Casey didn't sort the garbage right. He'd dump it into his barrel
even if someone's old car mats were in the mix, and the flames responded

with a brilliant green and deeply photogenic, resinous, yellow color,
and thick, black, nauseous smoke that the world would see in news reports from Haiti.

When my father saw the smoke from his office window,
he, who had taught me my skills, sent me out to fix up Casey's work.

III

I was excellent at fire-tending, excellent at mats, excellent on vacuum, steam gun,
window spray, side-window, back-window, checkout, cashier and driver.

And I was happy in that little corner of the yard, feeding customer tickets, newspapers,
lunch bags and magazines to the flames, staring down into the barrel,

feeling the heat on my face, the hairs on my arms crinkle, smelling them shrivel,
jabbing at the fire from above or stirring it through a pick-ax hole

with a length of rebar for a poker. I studied how the smoke would run
the length of tiny corrugations in a smoldering piece of cardboard

like little chimneys within the conflagration, or how moisture sweated out
of pages from the glossy magazines, and how quickly the fire could accept new material.

To keep it hot, I squirted gasoline from a ketchup bottle, and the flames
would scale the stream of gasoline and try to enter the bottle. (That happened once.)

I stared down into those fires in summer and winter,
whenever time permitted me the luxury of doing Casey's job,

and I felt, in my little garbage fire, all of the contentment that other men feel
at their crackling campfires a dozen miles from the nearest hiking trail

in the foothills of the Bitterroot Mountains because the Bitterroot Mountains
are someone else's mountains, someone else's car wash, and this was mine.

IV

My father and I were standing in the yard watching the garbage fire
one summer afternoon, when he told me he was thinking of selling the car wash.

He'd been on that corner forty years, and he knew my future lay elsewhere,
and he was going to turn his attention to finding a buyer.

And his voice had a tone less certain, not diminished, but gentler,
that I wouldn't hear again until his final days, like we were sitting

in a mostly empty bar with a ball game on the screen above the liquor bottles,
and the kind of friend a guy would be came sideways from his comments on the pitcher.

Our arms were crossed on our chests, and our legs were planted wide apart
because this is the way we stood. And there was a damp towel over my shoulder

because there was always a damp towel over my shoulder. And a car, I think a Lincoln,
pulled up to the entrance, and we watched Sam Tyler give the man a ticket.

And I said, "I could finish my class work and come down to help you in January."
And just like that, on the strength of nothing more than the intimacy in his voice,

I had agreed to give up my utterly free semester,
to come down from Syracuse and wash cars with him,

and I did it without him ever asking because I thought that he had.

VANESSA STAUFFER

Jean de Fiennes (The Young Man)

What did I think was going to happen?
We were gathered in the square
whoever could stand
We'd been starving seven months
I never knew what it meant
to be hungry like that: shoe leather
sticky porridges of parchment
the greasy horseflesh
I could see the gentle eyes
even as I swallowed

The king demanded six in exchange
for the rest to go not free exactly
but at least still breathing
The city was his for the taking
Had they scaled the walls
we couldn't have stopped them
weak as we were & stumbling
a maze with no center

no dream of deer grazing
the dewed hollow at dusk
stripping leaves from the sorrel
until the snap of a stick sent them back
to the saplings, black eyes fixed wide
muzzles quivered at the scent of milk
souring our breath
our hands filmed with tallow
slicking the string stretched tight
to the lip
the vane rustled soft against
the ear—

all we could hear
was the sound of the sun
splitting the earth in the fallow
fields left untended outside the walls
as we were dying inside them
how they cinched our sky
like a hood drawn over the head
as we wandered blinded & bent
I'd have laid down my sword
for a stale heel of bread

I didn't know that he knew
I didn't know that the martyrs meant nothing
to the fate of the living
Some symbol of his power
the crack of our necks ringing louder
than any clarion or gavel
I didn't know we were already

dead when the six started shucking
the fine clothes we still wore
pulling on the penitent's rags
looping the nooses around their necks
their narrow chests
their hair shorn off in tufts
drifting downy in the dust

It was like the old legends I loved
the men gathered to face a cruel god
a demon or monster
arming themselves for the battle
their faces grim & silent
as if they didn't know
they were heroes in a story being told
over & over & always
the ending a triumph
the beast slain
the city defended

At the gate Francois pitched forward
& fell
his eyes pinched shut
body or mind unable
One more they called
I saw myself step forward
through what was left of our people
lifting my chin as they settled the rope
heavy as an arm on my neck
the knot like a key
in the notch of my throat
I thought

someone would stop me
an old man offer to spare the young
but when the gates cracked open
when the wasted fields came into view

a snarl of winterweed & burdock
the careful rows grown thick & wild
under the aegis of the king
I saw the tableau of banner & tent
was breathing
was living & moving
singing & sharpening swords
stirring smoke from the coals
underneath a spit of game
They'd cut the copse of birch
& burned it green

I turned back to see
the gate swing shut like an eye
& knew I would die

What happened next
has no meaning
The queen begged for our lives
to be spared
for the sake of the child she carried
our deaths a bad omen

The king agreed
The child was born
strong & pink

We would hear him crying
as we worked the fields
coaxing them back into order
in the service of the king
little tyrant
who spared our lives

whose skull I would
stave with this shovel
given the chance

Translation Folio

KHAL TORABULLY

Translator's Introduction

Nancy Naomi Carlson

KHAL TORABULLY IS AN AWARD-WINNING poet, essayist, film director, and semiologist, born in 1956 in Mauritius, an island country located off the southeast coast of Africa, in the Indian Ocean. He is a descendent of migrant workers who came to Mauritius from India. Originally a Dutch colony, Mauritius was later ruled by the French, and finally by the British, before becoming independent in 1968. Half a million Indian indentured workers passed through the Aapravasi Ghat (immigration depot) in Port Louis between the years of 1849 to 1923. Many of the immigrants stayed in Mauritius to work in the sugar cane fields as a source of cheap labor, replacing the slaves after the abolition of slavery, while others were shipped to colonies all over the world.

Indentured workers were subject to exploitation during each step of the indenture process: signing up, traveling across the oceans, and settling in a foreign country. Many men and women were tricked into indenture through false promises. Transoceanic voyages were arduous and inhumane, and many died from illness or ill treatment along the way. Once delivered to the colonies, conditions continued to be nightmarish, with many laborers subject to harsh penalties (jail and/or a lengthened contract) for minor infractions.

Torabully has revisioned and transformed the meaning of the term "coolie," used in a pejorative way to describe mostly Indian and Chinese workers, to encompass the richness of transcultural exchanges. He coined the word "coolitude" in a way similar to how Aimé Césaire coined the term "negritude," imbuing the term with dignity and pride, as well as a strong and resilient multicultural identity and language. Torabully has developed a "poetics of coolitude" that gives voice to the oppressed and silenced. His work is recognized by UNESCO as a "vector of peace."

Torabully's language is inventive and fragmented, drawing on French, Mauritian Creole, English, Chinese, Urdu, and Arabic, as well as playful neologisms and rhymes. The humorous nature of his language underscores the tragic overtones of his subject matter. The music infused in the language (assonance, alliteration, and rhythm) also serves this purpose.

The translations in this selection illustrate Torabully's major themes. The poem "[As a guest at the bash]" describes how potential workers were plied with liquor to make them agree to indenture. "[My naked people]" focuses on the voyage, including the risk of beriberi to those confined to ships. "[Anjali]" tells of a sugar factory worker who was killed during a worker uprising in the 1930's, and alludes to the horrible working conditions of indentured sugar cane workers. Torabully's linguistic acrobatics are particularly in evidence in "[With my tottering soul]." For example, the last two lines of the poem are as follows: "Je suis à dire chair pure chair / chair par chair?" The literal meaning of these two lines is something like "I am to tell flesh pure flesh / flesh to flesh." The challenge was to find a way to maintain the staccato of the rhythm ("chair pure chair / chair par chair"), keep alliteration in the in-between words "pure" and "par," and stay fairly faithful to the meaning. In an effort to replicate the pattern and playfulness of these lines, I came up with the following: "I am, in truth, flesh fresh flesh— / flesh flush with flesh?"

The major translation challenge I faced with these texts was to honor their music without sacrificing meaning. Using my ear and my knowledge of linguistics, I used a sound-mapping technique to locate the most salient sound patterns of the original text (assonance and alliteration). I tried to approximate sounds (though not necessarily exact sounds, as some do not exist in English) in my translations. For example, the following was my sound map for the French poem "[Anjali]," with four of the five lines ending with the same vowel sound [ah]: "visage," "l'hamadryade," "mouroir," and "l'orage." In addition, the nasal sound [an] (which exists in French, but not English), is repeated three times in close proximity: "Anjali," "Ange," "étrange," which I've bolded. Another secondary sound pattern consists of past participles ending with "é": hâlé, salés, and troués, which I've underlined. The fourth line contains an abundance of alliteration (the sound "s"), as follows: "sucres," "salés," and "sueur."

For my translation, I was able to end four of the five lines with the same vowel sound, which I've italicized: "eyes," "riverside," "die," and "strife." For one of the secondary sound patterns, I used something similar to the French (the sound [ay]), which I've bolded below: "Angel," "strange," "place." The other secondary pattern of assonance is underlined: "star," "water," and "bronzed." I was able to replicate the French fourth line's pattern of s-sounds, as follows: "sugars," "salted" and "sweat."

Anjali pour tirer l'étoile à mon *visage*,
l'eau babille **Anjali** *l'hamadryade*.
Pour **Ange** <u>hâlé</u> **étrange** *mouroir*
à vos sucres <u>salés</u> de sueur:
O tes reins <u>troués</u> par *l'orage*.

Anjali to pull down the <u>star</u> to my *eyes*—
the <u>water</u> babbles Anjali, tree-bound nymph at the *riverside*.
For the <u>bronzed</u> **Angel**, a **strange place** to *die*
in sugars salted with sweat:
O your back riddled with holes from the *strife*.

To increase the musicality of this text, I also analyzed the rhythm of the original, which tends to stress the last syllable of each word—especially the last syllable of each line. Four of my five English lines follow that pattern by stressing the last syllable.

KHAL TORABULLY : Four Poems

[Anjali]

Anjali to pull down the star to my eyes—
the water babbles Anjali, tree-bound nymph at the riverside.
For the bronzed Angel, a strange place to die
in sugars salted with sweat:
O your back riddled with holes from the strife.

Translator's note: Anjali was a sugar factory worker killed during a worker uprising
in the 1930's.

[As a guest at the bash]

As a guest at the bash to launch the boat
I was already under the spell of the cane—
at the fair, at the marketplace
I was drugged with sugar, then thrown
into the ship's cargo hold.

[With my tottering soul]

With my tottering soul
I came to know how the sky began
as far back as its root-the-light.
Fiery designs
will always lick my porcelain.

Each scar is a clear dawn:
even flesh, even the sea.

For all unbreakable bodies
my wounds will no longer return
to my blood, save for the ocean's waves.

I am not crystal
from the India Trading Company.
I am human pollen
ready to tell of the cyclones again
in the screed of words.

My emblems are matrices, drums.
My beacon's in charge of the light of day.

And my eternity began
at the mooring lines of the very first sailor
on his glorious azure crossing:
not-to-be-uttered words, and all must be told.
I am human pollen
hitched to the helm of the sea.

I am, in truth, flesh fresh flesh—
flesh flush with flesh?

[My naked people]

My naked people, free of skin,
transplants of light!
And my lost legend
transfigures the island of stars.
Round bread slit bread
evokes my only home.
Beriberi
I know odysseys:
memory with no escape
is my path of sand.

translated from the French by Nancy Naomi Carlson

JYOTSNA SREENIVASAN

The Crystal Vase: Snapshots

REVATI STUMBLED AS SHE ENTERED the back door of her newly renovated kitchen-dining area clutching the thick stems of ivory tulips. The screen door clicked shut and she stopped to take a breath. The kitchen was redolent with the scent of baking cheese and garlic from the lasagna in the oven. Her husband, Bernard, ripped romaine lettuce at the counter.

"Hold these while I fill up the vase." She thrust the flowers at him.

He accepted the stems. "Calm down."

"I am calm." She climbed a stool to reach the cabinet above the fridge.

"I'm ready, Mommy." Her five-year-old daughter appeared at her side.

"You might be hot in that velvet dress." Revati stepped down with a tall, sleek rectangular glass vase pressed to her chest.

"I want to look beautiful for your friend Liz."

•

REVATI TURNED THE page of the photo album. "I remember taking this one in her bedroom, right before we went to a Girl Scout meeting." The background of the square Polaroid was almost black, and Liz's white face glowed like a ghost. She sat on her bed in a white blouse and pleated green skirt, her Girl Scout sash draped over her chest.

Bernard pointed to a mound of something on the bed behind Liz.

Revati leaned over the picture. "There were always piles of clothes everywhere. Sometimes she wouldn't know if they were dirty or clean."

"Sounds unpleasant," Bernard said.

Revati raised her eyes from the album. "It was a wonderful place. We could do anything we wanted and no one got upset. We'd eat things I wasn't allowed to at home. Cherry pie filling. We'd squirt whipped cream from a can all over it."

"I want to eat some!" Arsha ran to the refrigerator.

"Fortunately, we don't have any cherry pie filling." Bernard spooned Dijon mustard into a salad-dressing bottle, and added a stream of gold olive oil. "Sounds like her parents neglected her."

"No, Bernard. It was a cheerful house."

Bernard shook the dressing bottle vigorously. "Cheerful in what way?"

•

LIZ LEFT THE next morning after brunch. "I've got an early shift Monday," she explained. "You have such a nice family, Revati. I'll be really lonely now."

"You don't have to be lonely." Revati tried to be cheerful and reassuring. "Call me anytime."

"I'll send you the pictures," she said.

Liz didn't send the promised selfies they'd taken with her phone, but Revati received two text messages right away. The first one thanked her for the visit. The other message asked, "What does a person do with nothing to live four"

Revati, late for a meeting, replied quickly, "You sound desperate. Is that true?"

Almost immediately, Liz replied: "Not going to kill myself or anything"

•

"SHE MOVED AWAY when we were in sixth grade."

"So . . . about 30 years ago? What made her contact you all of a sudden?"

"She said she was looking for people from her past. She was looking for *me*, Bernard. She said I was the best friend she ever had." She held out her hands for the tulips and began trimming the stems.

"And . . . you invited her for the entire weekend."

"She's driving down all the way from Ohio."

"You could've just visited with her when you went up to see your parents."

"She's never been to DC before. I felt like she needed a vacation. You didn't have to leave work early today if you didn't want to." She adjusted the tulips in the water so the taller ones were in the center.

"I don't mind. It's just that I don't get why she's so important. You've never mentioned her before."

"We'd just arrived from India, and she was my first friend, back when other kids were put off by my accent." She set the tulips in their vase on the dining table. "I'll show you a picture of Liz."

•

AS REVATI CHANGED her clothes upstairs, the doorbell rang. "I'll get it!" Arsha screamed, running to the door.

"Look out the window and make sure it's Liz," Revati called, hurrying down. Arsha hadn't yet opened the door.

"Who is it?" Revati asked.

"Some old lady," she whispered.

Revati pushed aside the curtain on the door. Standing on the porch was a heavy-set, middle-aged woman with short graying hair, wearing a black jacket and jeans and carrying a large white shopping bag. Her face broke into a smile and Revati recognized, in the crooked teeth and crinkled eyes, something of her friend from long ago.

Before she opened the door, Revati bent to her daughter's ear. "Don't say that. Liz is not old," she murmured. "She's the same age as Mommy."

•

"ON WEEKENDS HER dad would sit in front of the TV watching *The Three Stooges* and drinking beer, and he'd laugh and laugh. Her mom had all these clothes from when she used to be thin, lingerie and cocktail dresses and high heels. Liz and I would go down to the basement and try them all on and do fashion shows for each other."

Bernard lifted an eyebrow. "Two ten-year-old girls modeling lingerie for each other?"

"What's lonjeray?" Arsha wanted to know.

"Bernard, it wasn't like that."

"What is it?" Arsha asked again.

"Nothing, sweetie. What I'm trying to say, Bernard, is that Liz's house was so different from mine."

"What're you getting so excited about?" he asked.

Revati lowered her voice. "Sorry. But do you get it? At my house, I never put a picture on the wall of my room without asking Mom first, and she'd usually say no because she didn't want to ruin the paint. The walls of Liz's room were plastered with posters and photos of her favorite musicians. She loved Michael Jackson. Madonna was getting popular. Liz told me which radio stations to listen to. We watched music videos and practiced moon walking."

"If you were such good friends, why'd you stop being friends?"

"She moved away." Revati shrugged. "Her dad left the family," she said to the photos in her arms. "Liz's mom moved everyone down to southern Ohio, to live with her mother. That was in the spring of sixth grade."

"So you could never play with her again?" Arsha's forehead wrinkled with worry.

Revati stroked her daughter's head. "At first we wrote a lot. And then . . ." her gaze drifted back to the photos. "My parents bought a house in a new subdivision in Kent, and in the fall I started seventh grade. I made new friends. I fit in with the other girls because of everything Liz had taught me."

"And you stopped writing," Bernard said.

"I remember her last letter at the beginning of seventh grade. She said her dad was having a baby with his girlfriend. She said her parents were getting a divorce." Looking up from the album, she quirked the corners of her mouth into a smile for

Arsha. "She said her dad brought her a puppy. And you know what, Arsha?"

"What?" Arsha asked breathlessly.

"She named her dog 'Revati.' I bet you didn't know that I had a dog named after me."

•

"You haven't changed a bit," Liz exclaimed, stepping inside and enveloping Revati in a hug, just as Liz's mother used to. "You're still slim. You've still got that beautiful shiny black hair I used to love so much. You could pass for 25, Revati. Really, you could." She set down the large white paper bag and struggled out of her jacket.

Revati accepted the jacket. "That's a pretty sweater," she offered in exchange. Liz wore a bulky top festooned with cables and bobbles.

"Thank you. Purple's my favorite color." Liz walked into the living room. "You have a beautiful house. I love wood floors. And good light from all the windows. When I heard you lived in a row house, I thought it would be dark."

"We're lucky to have a corner house," Revati agreed.

Liz craned her neck at the bookshelves. "Lots of books. I remember you were reading that *Little Women* series and every day at the bus stop you'd tell me the story, word for word."

"That must have been annoying."

"It was!" She broke into a peal of laughter. "I only put up with it because I loved you. Oh, I almost forgot." She lugged over the big white bag and lifted a large box out of it. "I thought you might like this."

•

"Yes, thank you, Revati," Liz said. "I did receive them."

"Have you looked at them?"

"I haven't had a chance yet."

"Let me know if I can help in any way."

Revati didn't hear from Liz after that. She texted her, but got no reply. Revati called her once more, and again Liz insisted she was "not so bad" and that she had not had a chance to look at the books or to call a counselor.

"Liz, I'm worried about you. Keep in touch, will you?"

"Sure."

"Call me anytime."

"Sure."

Revati waited for the phone to go silent before hanging up. She continued to hear Liz huffing.

"Are you still there, Liz?"

"You know, Revati, I thought—" She paused.

"Yes?"

"I thought about you so much when I was growing up in Marietta. Our friendship was the happiest thing I could remember. When I saw you again I thought I could—I don't know—capture that happiness again." She paused. "You can never go back again, can you?"

•

AT DINNER, LIZ ate slowly, chewing carefully and patting her lips with her napkin. She refused the wine Bernard offered. "I'm not much of a drinker," she said. "I wouldn't know a good wine from vinegar." Then she gave a short, deep chuckle. She sounded just like her mother. "Anyway, seeing the damage alcohol did to my family, I decided early on to avoid the stuff."

Revati felt Bernard's glance on her. How had she not realized that alcohol was a problem in Liz's family?

After a moment Revati asked Liz about her mother and younger sisters.

"Since I moved back up north I don't talk to them much anymore. I'm not really welcome at home." Liz poked a leaf of lettuce with her fork and placed it carefully in her mouth.

"Why not?" Revati asked.

She broke open a dinner roll and buttered it slowly. "I guess it was about three years ago," she said. "I was still living in Marietta. I was working at the hardware store and I had my own place. One day, out of the blue, Dad calls. He must've found me through directory assistance, because I certainly never tried to contact him. I hadn't seen him since he brought down my puppy. Mom was so depressed after the divorce and I sided with her.

"So as I said, Dad calls. He says he's sick, he has liver cancer, he has no one to take care of him. What about your wife? I ask. Well, it turned out she'd left him. So there he was, all alone up there in the hospital. He asks me to come up and see him. 'I know I haven't been a good father,' he says. 'Can you forgive me?'

"I felt sorry for him. For a couple years I was actually thinking I might want to try to find my Dad's other kids—my half-siblings. I didn't even know how many kids he had, or anything. I thought, that's no way to live, to not even know my own blood relations. I told my mom and sisters that I was going up north to see Dad, and they just about blew a fuse." Liz used her fork to drag pieces of arugula to the edge of her plate.

•

"SHE WAS 10 in this picture." The girl stood with hands resting on a wooden "fence" with a meadow scene as a backdrop. "All our school pictures that year had this same fence and backdrop."

Bernard stood behind Revati, arms around her waist and chin resting on her shoulder. "She doesn't look too happy."

"What d'you mean?" She elbowed him away.

•

SHE DIDN'T KNOW where to put the vase Liz had given her. A week after Liz's visit, it still sat on the coffee table in the middle of the living room. "It's so big and awkward," she told Bernard that night after dinner as they relaxed on the sofa with glasses of wine. She eyed the bulging vase encrusted with embellishments. "It won't fit on the fireplace mantle. If I leave it on that table, Arsha might knock it over."

"Do you like it?"

"It's way too fussy."

"Donate it to Goodwill, then."

"But Liz brought it to me with love. I can't give it away."

"Put it in a closet or something."

"I can't just hide it and forget about it, Bernard."

"I don't get why you feel so attached to her."

"Bernard. Listen." Her wine glass began to tip. Bernard took it from her and set it on the table. She looked down at the upholstery, tracing the pattern of leaves with a finger. "Here's how I found out that Liz was moving away." Her voice faded, and she cleared her throat. "One day she wasn't in school. I ran to her house as soon as I got off the bus, and rang the doorbell. No one answered, which was not unusual, so I just went in. Her mom was sitting in the recliner in the living room, crying. She was still wearing her nightgown. I'd never seen a grown woman sob like that. I went upstairs. Liz was in her sisters' bedroom, taking all the clothes out of the dressers and laying them in suitcases. She was crying too. She told me her dad had left and was living with another woman. She said they were going down to Marietta." Revati lifted her eyes to Bernard. "I . . . didn't know how to react. I ran home, upstairs to my room, and actually crawled under the bed." She covered her face with her hands. "I stayed there until my mother called me down to dinner."

Bernard rested his hand on Revati's knee. "You were young, too."

Revati reached for the crystal vase. It was cold and heavy. She cradled it on her lap.

•

THEY JOINED THE hordes of cherry-blossom viewers along the path around the Tidal Basin. After walking for about 20 minutes Liz needed to sit down. Arsha and Bernard continued on around.

"My knees bother me when I walk a lot," Liz said. Their bench was under a small tree thickly laden with white blossoms. They admired the pale pink lace of the trees around the shining pool, framing the white dome of the Jefferson Memorial.

"It's like a picture postcard," Liz said. She picked up a twig with two flowers that had fallen on the bench beside her, and twirled it slowly in her fingers. Crowds streamed past in both directions. Many were East Asian—perhaps Japanese—and South Asian.

"Everyone around here seems real educated," Liz remarked. "I'm going to be like that someday. I'm looking into training for a better job."

"What kind of job are you thinking about?"

"Oh, I don't know. In computers, maybe."

"That's neat, Liz."

"Yeah." Liz coughed. "I'm afraid I won't be able to learn anything new, though."

"Why not?"

"I'm pretty sure I have a learning disability. Don't you remember how hard it was for me to spell anything?"

"I figured spelling wasn't your thing." Revati curled and uncurled the loose end of her waist pack strap.

"I'm not a smart person like you, Revati. Learning doesn't come easy for me. I'm not looking forward to going back to school."

"But you don't like your job, right? So you want to go into something else."

"I like the job. The people I work with are real nice, and it's kind of fun to organize all the things we sell, the sheets and towels and little fixtures for your bathroom. When we get deliveries it's like Christmas. I love opening all the boxes. The part I don't like is having to send stuff back to the warehouse if it didn't sell. That seems sad to me."

"Overall, though, you like your job." She rolled the strap into a tight spiral.

Liz shrugged. "Sure."

"Then why do you want a different career?"

"I never thought this is all I'd be doing. I thought I'd be somebody. You know?"

"You are somebody." She released the strap and it unfurled. "You're the most compassionate person I've ever met. I don't know of anyone who has taken care of a dying father who abandoned them."

Liz waved her flowering twig in the air. "I don't even want to remember that. It was the most depressing thing I ever did."

"When you were a kid, what did you dream of doing?"

She coughed into her elbow and cleared her throat. "I had impossible dreams then. I wanted to be like all the famous people I ever heard about. I wanted to be like Florence Nightingale and Harriet Tubman. I wanted to do something that would make a big difference."

"I had no idea, Liz. You never told me."

"You were so much smarter than me. I was shy to tell you my dreams."

•

REVATI CARRIED THE step stool into the living room and climbed up, clutching Liz's vase under an arm. She managed to slide it onto the top of the bookshelf. There weren't any books up there since it was so hard to reach. When she descended and tilted her head to see the vase, she realized she'd probably never bother to get it down to use it. She didn't want to leave Liz's gift up there, forgotten, to get dustier and dustier. She stepped up again and grappled against the deeply etched hearts and doves for a fingerhold, trying to tip it onto her palm. It was heavy and slippery. She was afraid she'd cause it to fall and shatter. So she left it there in its unreachable, almost unseeable space.

•

THROUGHOUT THE WEEK, Revati received several messages a day from Liz. Sometimes she gave mundane news: "We got a shipment of towels in the strangest color" The actual color of the towels was not mentioned. Many of her messages asked unanswerable questions. One day it was: "What do you do when you have no one to love and no one loves you" Another day: "Do you believe in heaven and hell"

Revati put off replying. By Friday she still had not responded to Liz. "I guess your real busy" Liz wrote.

That evening Revati dialed Liz's number. After chatting for a few minutes, Revati got right to the point. "Liz, you sound depressed. You've been through a lot and you need help. I think it might be good for you to schedule an appointment with a counselor."

Liz huffed on the other end of the line. "It's not so bad."

•

REVATI LAY IN bed staring at the ceiling in the darkness. "Why's she so passive?" she asked Bernard. "It seemed like she wanted my help, but now she can't even take the time to look at a few books."

"Most people don't want to make changes in their lives." He put his arm around Revati and pulled her towards him for a kiss.

She pushed away. "I feel like I'm failing her again. If I were really her best friend, I'd do whatever it took to get her out of this rut. I'd go up there and make sure she got help. I don't want to, though. I don't want to take time away from my own life to support her that much. I don't love her enough for that. So I sent her a couple of books. She doesn't even like to read."

"She's got some pretty big emotional wounds. She's got to start loving herself first." Bernard reached for her. She rolled out of his grasp, sat up and put her feet on the floor.

"Where're you going?"

She didn't answer. She didn't even know what she was so upset about. Wasn't Bernard right? She was making too big of a deal about this.

She wandered into the hallway and found herself in Arsha's bedroom. The girl had kicked the covers into a corner and lay curled on the mattress, still in her jeans and T-shirt. On the floor was a half-made poster surrounded by markers with their caps off. Revati surveyed the scene. She ought to put away the markers. She ought to try to undress Arsha.

Instead, she sank onto the bed and leaned over her daughter. She put a hand on the tangled hair and bent to kiss her cheek, closing her eyes, trying to swallow the lump in her throat. She'd never visited Liz in Marietta—had never, in fact, been to the town at all—but in her mind she pictured Liz calling that dog of hers. Liz, still a skinny sixth grader with a blonde mullet, stood with her back to the viewer and looked to the horizon, where rolling green fields met a blue, cloudless sky. There was no dog in sight. Hands cupping her mouth, she called "Revati! RAY-vuh-tee!" The name echoed silently in the air.

MIKE WHITE

Inn

I know, I know
you have no more room.

We are all of us
full, filled.

No doubt in me
you foresee a long night
of blood and noise and worry

but for the tidy fact
of there being
no more room.

My good husband
who tends to the animal
is nine months afraid
and all but dead on his feet.

Understand—
I am not seeking
after your pity.

Strangely I know already
as in a dream given twice
how it all must end.

You will point me
down one road
and then another
because you know a place
out of the common way

where travelers
in difficult circumstances . . .

Do not look surprised.

You will snuff out the light
as we pass through the gate
and you will ascend
counting each stair to the room
in which your young wife keeps
your soft bed warm,

and when she half-asks
out of her sleep—*who?*—

you will answer
in the absolute dark
no one, love, no one.

MICHAEL HOMOLKA

On the Disappointing Nature of Spirituality

One day I will have to trade souls
with those whose voices
are the voices of God
Like flies the elect reproduce
and die   Saint John of the Cross
Teresa of Avila   having devoted
their lives to little huts
affixed to monastery walls
while we bat around the molecules
which most resemble afterlife
I work hard at soulfulness
but evolve barely at all
compared to Entertainment Weekly
types I turn my nose up at :
Amanda Seyfried   Ryan
Seacrest   Amanda   Amanda
Everyone has a soul or no one does
Buddha   so sentient and reflective
how could you think
to take credit for all my ideas?

T. R. HUMMER

Spat

As though I had expectorated into the soup tureen
   in the middle of dinner, I found myself an object
Of contempt in my own home, a hissing and a byword
   whereat the mob gathered in the street outside my window
Chanting in actual language, until even the dog packed up
   in solidarity and moved into a shelter. Was I in the wrong
Lane to navigate the closing of the gyres? I stood alone
   in the garden back of the house wearing a cast-off bathrobe
Cursing God and dying as I had been told I had to do.
   Even when the house collapsed, killing the children,
I was resigned. It was something I said. Or didn't say.
   It was a suicide bomber in my genes. There was a hole
In the pocket of the bathrobe I thought I should vanish into
   but the physics of the situation overwhelmed me. I wanted
To build my life over from the neutrinos up, or maybe to discover
   what really happens inside a black hole. Old and solitary,
Neither nobody nor a nation: In spite of everything, I was still
   curious and curiouser. At gunpoint, I could keep an open mind.

A Monument

I sit on the front porch in the Adirondack chair
   assuming the posture of Lincoln. A mockingbird
Passing by salutes me. I don't wave back. Even made of granite,
   I am petrified by fears for the soul of the nation.
I would pace the boards, but I am 19 feet tall
   sitting down! The overwhelming weight of me
Would destroy the front of the house. This is what it means
   to be mythological. If I were still alive,
I would whistle a hornpipe. Try puckering granite lips!
   I would smoke a cigar. I would summon Walt Whitman
From the ward of dismembered soldiers—we would play
   a game of whist. The country is rotting and all
The grownups are dead. If I stood, I would reach
   28 feet, not counting my stovepipe hat.
The day of reckoning arrives dressed in hazy sunrise,
   and I am helpless, locked in my own sheer mass.
Try striking a match with granite fingers, try shuffling cards.
   I should proclaim emancipation, I should write an address,
But my hands weigh 500 pounds apiece. It's a morning
   in August, and the mockingbird won't leave.
Perched on a branch, it does what mockingbirds do:
   grooms its feathers in the sunlight, pecks a sultry beetle.
It cares nothing for the rights of anyone; its freedom is its end. Glory
   Hallelujah, it warbles, all my stone eyes have ever seen.

HERA NAGUIB

Self-Portrait as a Khamba
in a Sabzi Mandi in Lahore

I've been here too long, falling on the building

    with broken windows   thrumming broken syllables

through cables   hanging like writhing veins.

Consider the driver slung in the backseat between rickshaw flaps.

Now he sees me,   now he doesn't.

        Consider the cars glimmering like the back of a whale.

Scabbed walls. Fissure.   How the city's refuse snags in my throat:

   a flaccid mynah, plastic bags, one banne frayed across the minister's grin.

The truth is I'll be here longer. Neither seen nor hidden.

   Once I wanted love: to blister awake, sing through

            your throbbing blue lung.

All my life, I have stood this still.

        I simply cannot see where to get to.

———————

Note:
In Urdu, *khamba* is an electrical pole, and *sabzi mandi* is a vegetable market.

PAIGE QUIÑONES

Still Life with Wadded Paper Towels

I wonder whether familiarity will take over.
Here, we are children who marvel

at a swirl of hair in sunlight,

the sparrow's cry for coitus.
And though I've touched a body not mine,

I'm surprised by your heat, how

I can perceive this desire so easily.
We are betrayed at our most animal.

Here, nothing is not lovely. The slatted light.

The accidental blood on my thighs, and
whatever I use to clean them.

We have been painted in hard lines

and I want to blur you out—a man
is most interesting where he doesn't belong.

So you play at negation, as though

we need that bruise made new again.
Someday I will hate you.

This is your way of saying: *I owe you nothing.*

JESSICA LYNN SUCHON

Ars Poetica with Post Traumatic Stress Disorder

Even the ashen ribs of oaks bear
      witness to the places I hide in the dark

space between streetlights, places
      the moon will not touch. It is always

like this, the way I clutch my knees
      with prayers that there will be a tomorrow

and colored prisms will still float on their backs
      in pools of gasoline, that the white

scab of ice will fracture and return
      to the dirt. Pray that somewhere within me

still lives the child who once believed
      her body and strawberries were made

from the same flesh.   The girl holds the soft
                    fruit between her palms, and waits for it

             to breathe or swell with pulse.
                    She upturns fistfuls of dirt and buries

             this secret deep within the earth, ignores
                    the worms that will tunnel through

             each chamber, the way the scarlet fruit
                    will soon collapse and fold itself again

             and again, into nothing. How long
      until my shadow dances free

from the tether of my feet, until up north
        my mother's lilies squeeze sunlight

between their leaved fingers,
        or I can call the shriveled branches

by a new name? How long until I forget
        nothing in this world belongs to us,

not even ourselves? Until I forget this
        whisper of air trapped in my lungs—

the way it tumbles, then hangs inside
        me, before scattering like minnows.

Translation Folio

CRISTINA RIVERA GARZA

Translator's Introduction

Julia Leverone

THE POEMS BY CRISTINA RIVERA Garza translated here come from her collection *Los textos del yo* [*The Texts of the I*]. In them she intellectualizes and conceptualizes the feminine gender and place and border crossing and writing and memory, using tacks of interpretation and evocation to both approximate and switch away from her ideas. She accrues senses of familiarity and estrangement, performing the same splits about which she writes.

•

IN "FIRST COUNSEL," Rivera Garza commences with a mouth that emits and engulfs. Here, the comparison of this with the Ganges brings forth the preconception held by Hindus that the waters promise absolution and release from consequence. Still, the poem tells us that words cannot carry a woman to such a paradise. Paradise, instead, only resides in memory, Rivera Garza tells us, which is pure language.

The poem straddles moments in memory that could bifurcate into pleasure or harm, or both things: shifting from the usual to unusual, menstruation to homicide, drug use and saving money to an unexplained Aeroméxico flight, all are potentials for many consequences that may or may not compound. Whether the menstruating girl enjoys her fertility or suffers on account of it, whether the flight leads to a successful trip or immigration or complicated, tainted versions of these, or inverts into more pain than ever anticipated, the moments delineated in the poem are pre-history. Pre-language, or outside of it, somehow always inexplicable.

By inviting us to read, to ask how it feels, the poet implicates us; as such, there will always exist the moment when we had not read or known, its own experience. This links us to the actors among the lines—we are them, they are us. We all become implicit.

•

"THE MANY LIES of the Place" begins with a permissibility for invention and even deception. Rivera Garza assigns agency to an unspecified (and so, freed) place for it to establish its own nature, and she is the one attempting to translate it. Its nature—here, we are given depictions of its sense, its feel, rather than identifying or typifying visual characteristics, which is how place is approached usually—is hardly fixed, though the poet's attempt to fix it in words for us ("I saw it everywhere; I created it everywhere") is a show of her admiration both for the place and for us (we have something to learn from it).

That about the place she "used to like to say" opens to a change in perspective of it over time; the lists, "placid, alive, rapid, sublime, yellow, resonant"; "allegory, metaphor"; "argument, hypothesis"; "enigma, vocation, style" make its nature multi-faceted and at once elusive, difficult to track. And what's more, these depictions are inherently abstract themselves, containing further abstractions and nuances, ranging from rhetorical and grammatical techniques to posing the place as flesh.

The crux of this poem, its crossing between the nature and experience of a place, emerges in two places where the poet describes describing the place (or translates translating) as when an enamored person—first, a man of a woman, and second, a transsexual man of a woman—observes his love. These two moves instruct us of her love for the place and also assigns a femininity to the place, but elsewise and with greater emphasis (for the double remove of describing describing/translating translating) of the gazes of these two lovers. Particularly that of the second, a much more informed, empathetic gaze, for the lover too was once woman, once belonged to or possessed a knowledge of experience that closes the translation gap between the lover and the loved. Purer, "with eyes open like plazas and bones cleared of people."

The end of this poem rests with an acceptance of the imprecision of beauty and symbolism. It rises on ritual (the wink and nod) and alights on new myth—the nineteen feet, the three threads, the eleven peaks have no provenance from any established mythology. It is thus turned individual, subjective, generative, and encouraging of such practices in the world; and the poem turns to be perhaps and after all about loveloss, learning and parting from someone or someplace or some mixture of both.

•

ACCORDINGLY IN "THE tell of the true addict" the sea is called out as a being. Rivera Garza explores the implications of this, especially those of the beach as borderland, and goes on to stage an example of a scene from memory, one peopled by herself and her family. The direst factor here is not exposure or the threat of becoming swallowed, but addiction (of course, here, speaking to a further application of the term); the cigarette is begged for, it sends the mother figure to another place; the smoking and drinking become an occasion marking the seeming end. Addiction to death and sacrifice are next cited as motivators for the transversal or oblique traveling implied over that beach, immigration. The glance of an instance of it, the desire and forward act, are much less permanent than the coldness of submerging across.

•

Rivera Garza was born in a place bordering to the US-Mexican national divide, on the southern side, in Tamaulipas, and now also lives and works in the northern-bordering San Diego area. This closeness and the flip of her residence are points of fascination and preoccupation here and elsewhere in Rivera Garza's work; and her probings of the delineations of experiences and identities complement and complicate the questionings she undertakes and asks us to undertake. As such, guided by this poet, we are and aren't accompanied, by her or by anyone to whom we might think we are linked by whatever similarity. And yet—despite the temerariousness or abstraction of Rivera Garza's conceptions of what makes us up, or place, or memory—she places her trust in connections. We must find ours.

CRISTINA RIVERA GARZA : Three Poems

the many lies of the place

I used to like to say it was beautiful

(and did as if describing a man describing a woman)

under the dusk of adjectives, looking to everything besides
the place was placid, alive, rapid, sublime, yellow, resonant . . .

In dissymboled cities the place was allegory, metaphor, burning comparison:
noun among nouns, an alcoholic and true thing.
A thing surrounded with smoke.

Within perfectly white rooms, in silent letters and nerved corners, the place
turned into argument, hypothesis, immoral object of study.

On unpossessed nights the place changed into flesh under the mist,
adolescent vision, masturbatory mania.

There were streets on which, at certain times and only on high terrain, the place
    became like a parenthesis, lapsus linguae, interfering postscript.

In the few truly moving books there were paragraphs that brought it forth as
    enigma, vocation, style.

I saw it everywhere; I created it everywhere.

But mostly I liked to say that it was beautiful

(and did it like a woman made a man in love with a woman)

with eyes open like plazas and bones cleared of people.

Hopeless
within the docility of a certain catholic doom crossed by mosquitoes

the place *was* beautiful

(or rather: the place was the investigation where the word *beautiful* crept with its
  nineteen blue feet)

and then the left eye gave the required wink and the nod producing rimmel and
  absinthe

once upon a time

and the man made woman trained upon the three threads of legend, the eleven
  stings of wonderment

there was a time

a place beautiful because it was mine.

First counsel: Do you want to know how it feels?

Avid reader: they don't feel a thing.

The woman pulls out her earrings and submerges into the Ganges of the mouth
  without feeling anything.
The man who says yes to the drugs doesn't feel anything.
The assassin squeezes more and then a little more without feeling anything.
Those who put bombs in convents don't feel anything.
The girl observes the dark little lines of menstruation between her thighs without
  feeling anything.
Those who open an account in a bank for the first time don't feel anything.
The lady who leaves her country on a dawn Aeroméxico plane doesn't feel anything.
Passion and crime always happens after the fact.
Panic and malice occur one moment later, one era later.

Avid reader: only in memory (which is pure language) do we feel.

the tell of the true addict

At times the Sea of the North transformed into a blanket
and it had to be regarded as some other being.

At times you could put it over your shoulders
like something very worn or loved, and feel, drawing from
unspoken elements, its heat or its displacement.

At times it was possible to sit on its shore,
peacefully. And turn into a sudden sculpture or a mindless
cloud. Or sand with edges.

Anything could happen there, in truth. At times you had
to fly over it as you would a disaster. Or move away as you would
from an epidemic. Or resign yourself like to a sickness.

On more than one occasion we saw the unexpected and no less
natural way that from the water the head
of Concha Urquiza emerged

—But if you're dead, we reminded her quickly.

And she, without paying us attention, interrupted whatever
commentary to ask us, with that desperate tell
of the true addict, for a cigarette.
For the love of God. For what you love most. And once
the first suck had been taken—deep, with pleasure, all of her
in another place—and once she had made the gray mouthful
disappear in the air, the smoke of artifice, then
she asked for a towel.

—You have no idea how cold it was, she assured us
without daring to glance back. When she registered
the surprise in our faces she wasn't able to contain her laughter.

—What? You're like the rest who think that The Submerged
never get cold?

We were like them, surely. And because of this, we kept
a guilty and timid silence, with our eyes downcast.

—At least, she murmured in a peace-making tone, you
could offer me a little wine.

Then, without us asking her, without
us expecting it at all, The Submerged raised
her glass and toasted and sucked avidly
on her cigarette, all at once, all as if
she didn't have time left or as if her time
was ending, and she stayed like us, sitting
peacefully on the sandy shore of the Sea of the North,
resigned before the sickness of the water and flying
over the disaster with the Oblique Glance from which she has died
more than once, from which she still hasn't ceased dying
or to which, dying, she recurs like a true addict, with that for-the-love-
of-God, that cruel martyr's tell, that of a beheaded princess.

translated from the Spanish by Julia Leverone

IRA SUKRUNGRUANG

When We Are Done Vanishing

BEFORE, I COULD DISAPPEAR IN a mound of laundry, vanish into the dark of a closet. I could make myself a shadow of the city. Now, I'm always found. There are benefits to being. There are benefits to disappearing.

•

When I was a boy, I enjoyed sitting in a dark closet, atop my father's briefcase of important things. I would wave my hand in front of my face and not see my hand. I would wiggle my fingers and not see my fingers. That dark was a comfort. Out there was too much light, blinding.

•

In the old neighborhood in Chicago, the Hide-n-Seek games were intense. We hid in outrageous places—inside dumpsters with rats and the remnants of rotted lunches, in concrete churners at construction sites, in hollowed-out cars. One time someone went into a rusted refrigerator. One time someone descended down a chimney. There were two rules: we had to stay in a one-block radius, and after fifteen minutes, we had to emerge.

•

In Monica Wood's short story, "Disappearing," the main character, a 300lb. woman, starts swimming to lose weight. She loses and loses and loses. Her physical self. Her sanity. She desires to become nothing. When confronted, she says, "I'm disappearing . . . and what can you do about it, not a blessed thing."

•

When my son wakes, after his little stretches and yawns, he faces me and pinches the hell out of my nipple. His fingernails are sharp; most fifteen-month old nails are. He pinches and never takes his eyes off my face. I put a hand to my mouth. Stifle the scream. Undeterred, my son pinches again. Still I do not give in. Another pinch. This time I let out a scream that trails into breathy laughter. My son breaks a smile, teeth beginning to fill his mouth. He pinches once more. We scream together.

•

In my travels, I jump from city to city, anonymous. I am without a name. Anonymity strides alongside me in the airport, matches the click in my steps. Anonymity sits beside me in the cab. When the driver asks what I'm doing in the city, like he did this last weekend, Anonymity answers for me: "Nothing. Just disappearing for a bit."

•

In Lewis Carroll's *Alice in Wonderland*, when Alice plummets down the hole, she is gone from the world she knows and enters a world without sense. The world without sense makes her real. Gives her purpose. The world without sense is carved from the surrealistic part of the brain, that part that creates monsters and ghosts and talking furniture.

•

Since I was old enough to speak, my family taught me about the existence of ghosts. My father in particular was exceptional at telling ghost stories. In many of the stories, ghosts made themselves known. There was never a ghost who didn't want to be found. This gave reason for the mysterious footsteps in the attic. The floating candlestick down a long corridor. The whisper mistaken for wind.

•

In Major Jackson's poem "On Disappearing," the speaker repeats the line, "I have not disappeared," and it is a reminder—a mantra, perhaps—of the tenuous grip the speaker has on life. Yet this one line, presented in a couplet, stills me into understanding: "In my children, I see my bulging face / pressing further into the mysteries."

•

In Chicago Hide-n-Seek games, when you were found the seeker punched you in the arm as hard as he could, sometimes leaving knuckle-sized bruises.

•

There was a time—there were many times—when I did not go out of the house. There was a time—there were many times—when I thought of vanishing. I thought a lot about it. I think about it now, and it sends me looking for something to locate me in the present world.

•

I love our morning nipple-pinch ritual. I know it will disappear, and only the memory of it will linger. I love it because my son finds me in the most physical way possible. He finds me and says you are mine.

•

When my boy was 6-months old his hands fascinated him. He stared at them. Wiggled his fingers. Opened and closed his hands. He was seeing himself into being. He was realizing the body was substantial; the body was what located him in the world. Once he caught me spying on his finger intrigue. He smiled and thrust his hand up, as if to say, *Look, Dad. Look what I've found.*

•

I was not good at Hide-n-Seek. I was usually found first—except one time. But really, I just don't think I tried that hard.

•

When Alice returns to the real world, she emerges a different girl. A stronger, more confident girl. "It's no use going back to yesterday, because I was a different person then."

•

I'm learning to exist. Most of my life, I've lived in my mind. I play out life in my vacant stare. Beneath that stare, my brain is living multiple me's. And those multiple me's are doing multiple me things, while my body occupies space. It feels like that boy in the closet without a body, the body in the dark without form.

•

My son possesses the same look—that faraway gaze. Sometimes he stares at a wall or the ceiling, his mouth slightly parted. When I call his name, the two syllables rolling off my tongue, he doesn't answer. I keep saying his name, like the trill of a bell. Only touch brings him back.

•

Once I hid at the top of an apple tree. When I moved or shifted my weight, apples dropped and bruised on the concrete below. I stayed as still as possible. The seeker moved underneath me, like a burglar. His eyes darted back and forth. From above I could see his swiveling head of blond hair. I was twenty or so feet above him. I could spit on his head. I held my breath and became not a boy but a tree. He never looked up. After a bit, he moved on. I was never found.

•

The reason I'm thinking about disappearing is because disappearing happens. Your father is there and then he is not. Your friend is there and then she is not. You are here and then you are not. Eventually no one will look for us.

•

My son loves to put things over him. Blanket and sheets. He thinks he has vanished. I say, "Where's my boy? Where's my boy?" He giggles, a trembling sheeted ghost.

•

And then he whips the sheet off and there, all smiles, is my boy.

•

At some point, I will be gone. A memory. Will I be nothing then?

•

I put the covers over my son, so he becomes a lump in the bed. Only his giggles tell me he is part of the world.

•

Another one of my son's favorite games is disappearing behind curtains.

•

My favorite game: finding him.

CHELSEA WAGENAAR

September Psalm

—Valparaiso University

It's summer's last call,
the sky electric coral in the evenings,
then ashen pink, then a final pale pucker
as bats dart beneath lights.
This is the hour of the erasers,
come to ghost the classrooms
with a little humming, some water
sloshed from a pail,
and the great unwriting begins.
They absolve midterm dates,
cancel Gettysburg, erode the ribs
of the human skeleton.
They unstack the kindling
of the music staff, halve the half notes,
unconjugate *cantar*.
The erasers thumb their rosary
of rooms and walk out
beneath a chalk moon.
The sky is a sill of dust.
Beneath it, the stadium shudders
with a primal chorus,
which rises toward the towering lights,
where a thin cloud of moths
clots against a brilliance
they can neither resist nor keep.

JENNY BOYCHUK

Doctor's Appointment, After Her Death

Do you have nightmares?

> Yes, it was long ago that a cloaked woman
> asked me to believe in the wind.
> None of her angels have arms.

What about insomnia?

> A window left
> gaping. Summer thunder
> crackles, thrusts against land.

An impaired short-term memory is common.

> But she remembered me
> before I could remind myself:

Have you had any thoughts of suicide?

> the butterfly digests itself before
> it is reborn. Risks it all. Then, a single
> swipe of cat claw to its yellow wing.

The grieving process can vary—was the death expected?

> As a girl, I would arrange an audience
> of dolls and plastic horses. Together,
> my miscarried brother and I
> would rehearse

And there is a family history of mental illness?

forgiveness. There are certain things
I expected to inherit. Eyes that flood
with spring's run-off. A gold cross.
A green felt coat—

but the bottles of white pills
sewn into its pockets, are they mine?

How long have you had trouble swallowing?

Half-Moon Elegy

—in memory of F. B.

What's left when you halve
every memory of our feet

dipped in the icy Columbia River,
daring the other to hold still

a little longer—cold feet
or a cold tongue? If I halve

the sobs your mother released
into the phone when she explained

how your truck had rolled,
you get the man I'm unbuckling

for in San Juan del Sur—
our rum-glossed lips, half-moon

bite marks on either side of his
forearm: a fullness only possible

with someone I could never
love. Outside, the ocean cradles

fishing boats. Bull sharks keep
the night watch beyond the shallows.

All his weight against me. I keep
thinking of you. Even if I halve

the memory of us & the river,
it's still winter, & you're still

going to die. In the dark, I coil
into mattress spring thinking

of the moon: a split lip over the bay
—how, like you, each night

it pushes the sun away.

COREY VAN LANDINGHAM

Great American Ball Park

They all throw harder now.
This close, the catcher's mitt snaps
against each fastball. The game—
late summer, playoffs set—doesn't
matter. The stadium nearly empty.
Seats we could never afford.
We wait for the ump to decide
our future, lean closer,
spill the bag of popcorn. We strip
spun sugar from its paper
cone. Kingdom of kiss cams
and beer-damp foam fingers.
This close, we can't see the sun
setting over the Ohio. Here,
before Christ, buffalo crossed
searching for the great salt springs
of the South. This close
the players seem, entering
their dugouts, like they're falling
from some sharp cliff.
Aisle vendors shout their last
ascents and we're alone—
top of the ninth—no more cold beer
delivered unto us. A hero stands
for our applause. He needs it
(all in the eyes) the way we need
a win against the rich North
team in blue, need to see ourselves
on the big screen proving
our devotion. It is nearly
dark, and we're striking out,
are sturdy in our decline. How
have we not already died out

among the other divine
heartland beasts? All evening
we've hunted spaces where no man
stands. The last pitch—reckless,
sentimental—singing out, out
of the stadium, heading
toward the river. Boys and girls
of America, can you hear it?
Kingdom of foul balls
and maple that might very well
break. We're close enough
to receive its shards.

JOHN KOETHE

Tempting Fate

I know it means to take a risk,
But I prefer the semi-pun:
That we're seduced by the idea
Of helplessness—that whatever we do,
Our ends are preordained, and once begun
Our lives proceed to their conclusions
With the impersonal precision of a well-made play.
I dislike drama. Whatever brought me here—
Whatever left me here—remains unwritten, waiting
For its masterwork to be completed, when no one
Cares about it one way or another anymore.
What is the deep attraction of the fantasy
That everything just happens, nothing is meant,
And whatever you do you're simply what you are?
It isn't anything experience confirms,
But something we're determined to believe:
That instead of equaling the sum of his revisions,
A person amounts to what he leaves, which disappears.

I don't believe a word of it. When on the opposing side
Of the ledger I calculate the years I've spent preparing—
Or really, not preparing—for my fate, all I feel is gladness:
Not for anything I've done or what I am, but for the underlying
Miracle that magnifies my life and let my world begin.
I owe myself to accidents: when in the course of human
Randomness the stars were in alignment or across a crowded
Room two destinies combined, nothing in an eternal sense
Occurred, yet it left me as I am: a ridiculous person
Worried about bills, gasoline mileage, a new car, grateful
For the presence of a present accentuated by sadness,
Moving without deliberation to the measures of his heart.
This cheerfulness (or is it just indifference?) isn't a façade,
And yet it's fragile, prone to crumbling at the dropping of a hat.

Sometimes in the midst of life—in an airplane, standing on a sidewalk,
At home and leafing through a magazine—I suddenly feel alone,
With a sense of sheer contingency, and I feel afraid.

I think rhetoric is glorious, unleashing meanings
That didn't exist before, but I hate its need to make things up.
Take this poem: reading a biography of James Merrill,
I felt inflected by a germ of words. I'm in New York, saw JA
After five whole years, talked about JM, JS, JY, JG,
Without any spirits intervening. DK was angry as usual,
Which made me feel at home. How can anybody live here?
It costs too much, everyone is ugly, everyone is beautiful,
All of them have stories. People don't have stories,
Just lives that no one wants to hear about. I like people
In small doses, but when I look up at the buildings and blue sky,
They're reduced to their initials, which stand for their lives.
What I like are poems with people's names in them,
Where the reality behind those names remains unfinished,
Waiting on that day that never comes, when we pronounce ourselves
And meet one another as we are. Meanwhile we live in abeyance,
Posting brief bulletins to remind each other of who we are—
Here I am, won't you friend me, don't forget to write—
If only for the sake of someone's sudden recognition
Of someone else, existing in the creases, living far,
Far away, beyond imagination, which is par for the course.
Hope to read about you soon. D, you know who you are.

BENJAMIN S. GROSSBERG

Missed Connections

I remember the 1970s, which is like
adults, when I was a kid, remembering
the 1930s, an arm reaching back
into pre-history, the world before Hitler—
grainy, black-and-white, soundless,
and the movement all herky-jerky
like stop-motion animation,
something from the '70s, for example,
that I remember. Think Sinbad
fighting enormous scorpions.
But that older older world had
no scorpions. Back then, the moon
was manifestly a cut out, and rockets
lifted on guywire you could see
against a black background.
When people spoke, a placard flashed
their sentences, and even *The End*
was signified with a flourish.
That's how we'll remember
the '70s one day, if we don't already,
a lime-green Oldsmobile, rust-
riddled, cracked vinyl seats with
wedges of yellow foam poking through.
There we sit, three brothers and I, wedged
arm against arm, zipped into dark
blue parkas that even in memory
sport a patina of filth. It's snowing,
but we've just pulled into a rest stop
with a long counter. Large lights
hang down—orange, yellow, and green
globes—and a waitress is about to
bring us each half a doughnut.
Meanwhile, miles north, my

grandmother recalls Poland, her
socialite youth, posing
with her sisters for its one
extant photograph, still scallop-
edged and fine. Her legs cross
high at the knee, and pearls
the Nazis will later pocket, dangle
nearly to her lap. Someone's
scrawled a year—1927—on the back,
crossing the seven like a T.
A puff of smoke still rises
from the flash, and behind her,
the curtain, florid backdrop, parts
like those in old cinemas.
Let's project 2017 there, writ large—
a circle made of two arrows, head
to tail, chasing each other,
our moment's own ouroboros,
as we wait for the next clip to load.

Bios

FARAH ALI is the recipient of the *Colorado Review* 2016 Nelligan Prize for short fiction. Her work has appeared in *Ecotone*, *J Journal*, and *Versal*. She lives and writes in Dubai, UAE.

JENNY BOYCHUK's work has appeared in *Best New Poets 2016*, *Malahat Review*, *Prairie Fire*, *Salt Hill*, and elsewhere. She lives in Ann Arbor, Michigan.

ZOË BRIGLEY, originally from Wales, is a visiting assistant professor at Ohio State University. She has published two poetry collections—*Conquest* (Bloodaxe, 2012) and *The Secret* (2007)—and her third collection, *Hand and Skull*, is forthcoming in the UK in 2019.

ERIKA JO BROWN is the author of the poetry collection *I'm Your Huckleberry* (Brooklyn Arts, 2014) and co-editor of *Beatrice Hastings: On the Life & Work of a Lost Modern Master* (Pleiades, 2016). She is a recipient of the Truman Capote Literary fellowship through the Iowa Writers' Workshop and currently works at the University of Texas MD Anderson Children's Cancer Hospital through WITS.

JAMES BYRNE is a co-editor of *Atlantic Drift: An Anthology of Poetry and Poetics* (ARC, 2017) and the author of *Everything That Is Broken Up Dances* (Tupelo, 2015). He was a Stein Fellow at New York University and now teaches poetry at Edge Hill University near Liverpool, England.

VAHNI CAPILDEO is the author of *Measures of Expiration* (Carcanet, 2016), which won the 2016 Forward Prize, and *Venus as a Bear* (2018). She held the Judith E. Wilson Poetry Fellowship and the Harper-Wood Studentship at Cambridge and is currently a Douglas Caster Cultural Fellow at the University of Leeds.

A recipient of grants from the NEA and the Maryland State Arts Council, **NANCY NAOMI CARLSON** is the author of three books of poetry and 5 books of translations, including, recently, her translation of René Char, *Hammer with No Master* (Tupelo Press, 2016), which was a finalist for the 2017 CLMP Firecracker Award in Poetry, and her translation of Abdourahman Waberi's *The Nomads, My Brothers, Go Out to Drink from the Big Dipper* (Seagull, 2015), which was a finalist for the Best Translated Book Award.

EMILY J. COUSINS' poems have appeared in *Another Chicago Magazine, The Collapser, Denver Quarterly,* and *The Laurel Review.* She lives in Denver.

MARTIN DYAR's collection *Maiden Names* (Arlen House, 2013) was shortlisted for the 2014 Pigott Poetry Prize, and he has won the 2009 Patrick Kavanagh Award and the 2001 Strokestown International Poetry Award. His work also appears in the Penguin anthology *Windharp: Poems of Ireland Since 1916* (2015). He currently holds the 2018 Irish Arts Council writer-in-residence fellowship at the University of Limerick.

ELAINE FEENEY is the author of three poetry collections: *Rise* (Salmon, 2017), *The Radio Was Gospel* (2013), and *Where's Katie?* (2010). She teaches at St. Jarlath's College in Tuam, Ireland.

Co-founder of *Field* magazine, STUART FRIEBERT is the author of numerous books of poetry, most recently *Decanting: Selected and New Poems* (Lost Horse, 2017), as well as the recent prose volume *First and Last Words: Memoirs & Stories* (Pinyon, 2017). He has also translated many poetry collections, most recently *Scant Hours: Selected Poems of Elisabeth Schmeidel* (Pinyon, 2018) and *Votives: Selected Poems of Kuno Raeber: From the Literary Remains* (Lost Horse, 2017).

BENJAMIN S. GROSSBERG is the author of four poetry collections, most recently *An Elegy* (Jacar, 2016) and *Space Traveler* (U. of Tampa, 2014). He has received individual artist grants from the states of Connecticut and Ohio and teaches at the University of Hartford.

MICHAEL HOMOLKA's book *Antiquity* (Sarabande, 2016) won the 2015 Kathryn A. Morton Prize in Poetry. His work has appeared in *The New Yorker, Ploughshares,* and *Agni.* He currently teaches high school in New York City.

T. R. HUMMER is the author of numerous books of poetry, most recently *After the Afterlife* (Acre, 2018) and *Skandalon* (LSU, 2014), as well as two books of criticism, most recently *Available Surfaces* (U. of Michigan, 2012). The recipient of Guggenheim and NEA Fellowships and the Richard Wright Award for Artistic Excellence, he lives and writes in Cold Spring, New York.

CHRISTOPHER KEMPF is the author of *Late in the Empire of Men* (2017), which won the 2015 Levis Prize from Four Way Books. He is the recipient of a Pushcart Prize, a National Endowment for the Arts Fellowship, and a Wallace Stegner fellowship from Stanford University. He lives and writes in Chicago.

VICTORIA KENNEFICK's debut pamphlet *White Whale* (Southword, 2015) won the Munster Literature Centre Fool for Poetry Chapbook Competition and the Saboteur Award for Best Poetry Pamphlet. Her poems have appeared in *Poetry*, *Poetry Ireland Review*, *The Stinging Fly*, and elsewhere. The recipient of a Next Generation Artist Bursary from the Arts Council of Ireland, she lives in Tralee in County Kerry, Ireland.

The recipient of two NEA fellowships, **DAVID KEPLINGER** is the author of five collections of poetry, most recently *Another City* (Milkweed, 2018) and *The Most Natural Thing* (New Issues, 2013). His translations include Jan Wagner's *The Art of Topiary* (Milkweed, 2017) and two books by Carsten René Nielsen: *House Inspections* (BOA, 2011) and *World Cut Out with Crooked Scissors* (New Issues, 2007). He directs the MFA Program at American University in Washington, D.C.

L. S. KLATT is the author of four poetry collections, including *The Wilderness After Which* (Otis, 2017), *Sunshine Wound* (Parlor, 2014), and *Cloud of Ink* (U. of Iowa, 2011), which won the Iowa Poetry Prize. He teaches at Calvin College in Grand Rapids, where he was recently Poet Laureate.

The recipient of the Lenore Marshall Prize and the Kingsley Tufts Award, **JOHN KOETHE** is the author of numerous poetry collections, most recently *The Swimmer: Poems* (FSG, 2016) and the forthcoming *Walking Backwards: Poems 1966–2016* (2018). He is Distinguished Professor of Philosophy Emeritus at the University of Wisconsin-Milwaukee.

JULIA LEVERONE's chapbook *Little Escape* (JMWW, 2017) won the Claudia Emerson Chapbook Award. Her translations of Rivera Garza's poems have also appeared recently in *Blue Lyra* and *Gulf Coast*. Her translation of Paco Urondo's *Fuel and Fire*, is forthcoming from Dialogos Press. She is an editor for *Sakura Review*.

COREY MARKS is the author of *The Radio Tree* (New Issues, 2012) and *Renunciation* (U. of Illinois, 2000), which won the National Poetry Series. He is a poetry editor for *American Literary Review* and his work has appeared in *New England Review*, *Poetry Northwest*, *Ploughshares*, and *Southwest Review*. He teaches at the University of North Texas.

KATHLEEN McGOOKEY is the author of three poetry collections, most recently *Heart in a Jar* (White Pine, 2017) and *Stay* (Press 53, 2014), and she has translated *We'll See: Poems by Georges L. Godeau* (Parlor, 2012). Her work has appeared in *Crazyhorse*, *Field*, *Indiana Review*, *Ploughshares*, and elsewhere. She lives and writes in Middleville, Michigan.

BECKA MARA McKAY is the author of *A Meteorologist in the Promised Land* (Shearsman Books, 2010) and has translated three book of fiction from Hebrew, most recently Alex Epstein's *Lunar Savings Time* (Clockroot, 2011). Her poems and translations have appeared in *ACM*, *American Letters & Commentary*, *The Iowa Review*, *Third Coast*, and elsewhere.

JUAN MORALES is the author of *The Siren World* (Lithic Press, 2015), and the forthcoming *The Handyman's Guide to End Times* (U. of New Mexico, 2018). He is a CantoMundo Fellow, the editor of Pilgrimage Press, and Chair of the Department of English & Foreign Languages at Colorado State University-Pueblo.

MANUELA MOSER's work has appeared in *Tender*, *Tangerine*, and the anthology *The Future Always Makes Me So Thirsty: New Poets from the North of Ireland*. She lives in Belfast and runs *The Lifeboat,* a reading series and small poetry press.

Originally from Lahore, Pakistan, **HERA NAGUIB** holds an MFA from Sarah Lawrence. Her poems appear in *Beloit Poetry Journal*, *Prairie Schooner*, *Tinderbox*, *World Literature Today*, and elsewhere.

CARSTEN RENÉ NIELSEN is a well-known Danish poet who lives in Aarhus. For more information, see page 35.

KATHRYN NUERNBERGER is the author of two poetry collections—*The End of Pink* (BOA, 2016), which won the James Laughlin Award, and *Rag & Bone* (Elixir, 2011)—and a book of essays, *Interviews with the Romantic Past* (Ohio State UP, 2017). She teaches at the University of Minnesota Twin Cities.

CONOR O'CALLAGHAN is the author of five poetry collections—most recently *Live Streaming* (*Gallery*, 2017) and *The Sun King* (2013)—and the novel *Nothing on Earth* (Black Swan, 2016). Born in Newry in County Down and raised in Dundalk in Ireland, he teaches at Sheffield Hallam University.

PAUL OTREMBA is the author of two poetry collections, *Pax Americana* (Four Way, 2015) and *The Currency* (2009). Recent poems have appeared in *Oversound*, *West Branch*, *The Kenyon Review*, *Waxwing*, and *West Branch*. He teaches at Rice University and teaches in the Warren Wilson low-residency MFA program.

PAUL PERRY is the author of five poetry collections, most recently *Gunpowder Valentine: New & Selected Poems* (Dedalus, 2014). He has also published several co-authored novels under the name Karen Perry. He teaches at University College Dublin.

MICHAEL PONTACOLONI's poems have appeared or are forthcoming in *The Adroit Journal*, *Denver Quarterly*, *Mississippi Review*, *New Ohio Review*, and elsewhere. He lives in Hartford, Connecticut, and runs a small vintage clothing company.

PAIGE QUIÑONES is a PhD fellow in poetry with the Center for Mexican American studies at the University of Houston. Her work has appeared or is forthcoming in *Barrow Street*, *Muzzle Magazine*, *McSweeney's*, *Quarterly West*, and elsewhere.

Born in Matamoros, in Mexico, prolific poet, fiction, and essayist CRISTINA RIVERA GARZA teaches at the University of Houston. For more information, see page 149.

SAM RIVIERE is the author of the poetry collections *Kim Kardashian's Marriage* (Faber, 2015) and *81 Austerities* (2012), as well as several limited-edition publications including *True Colours* (After Hours Ltd, 2016) and *Standard Twin Fantasy* (Egg Box, 2014), and a selection of his work appears in *Penguin Modern Poets 5* (2017). *Safe Mode* (Test Centre, 2017), an "ambient novel," is his first work of fiction. He lives in Edinburgh and runs the micropublisher If a Leaf Falls Press.

CAITLIN ROACH's work appears or is forthcoming *Handsome*, *The Iowa Review*, *Poetry Northwest*, and *Prelude*. She teaches at the University of Nevada, Las Vegas.

ARTHUR RUSSELL is the author of the chapbook *Unbent Trumpet* (Nutley Arts, 2017). His work has appeared in *Bettering American Poetry*, *Brooklyn Anthology*, *Prelude*, *The Red Wheelbarrow*, and elsewhere. He lives in New Jersey.

FRANCIS SANTANA is a Dominican-American writer and educator from New York City. His work has appeared or is forthcoming in *Blackbird*, *Indiana Review*, *Ninth Letter*, *Rattle*, and elsewhere.

STEPHEN SEXTON lives in Belfast where he teaches at the Seamus Heaney Centre for Poetry. His poems have appeared in *Granta*, *Poetry London*, *Best British Poetry 2015*, and elsewhere. His pamphlet *Oils* (Emma, 2014) was the Poetry Book Society's Winter Pamphlet Choice, and he won both the 2016 National Poetry Competition and the 2018 Eric Gregory Award. A first book will be published by Penguin in 2019.

LORNA SHAUGHNESSY has published several poetry collections, most recently *Anchored* (Salmon, 2015) and *Witness Trees* (2011). She is also a translator of Hispanic poetry; her most recent translation, *The Disappearance of Snow* (Shearsman, 2012), by Galician writer Manuel Rivas, was shortlisted for the Popescu Prize. She lectures in Hispanic Studies at NUI Galway in Ireland.

EMILY SKAJA's poems have appeared in *Best New Poets*, *Blackbird*, *Crazyhorse*, *Field*, and other journals. She serves as the Associate Poetry Editor of *Southern Indiana Review* and lives in Cincinnati, Ohio.

MOLLY SPENCER's poetry has appeared or is forthcoming in *Blackbird*, *Georgia Review*, *Gettysburg Review*, *New England Review*, among others. She is Poetry Editor at *The Rumpus* and lives in metro Detroit.

JYOTSNA SREENIVASAN's novel *And Laughter Fell From the Sky* was published in 2012 by HarperCollins. Her short fiction has been published in numerous literary magazines, and she has written children's novels and nonfiction reference books. The recipient of an Artist Fellowship Grant from the Washington, DC, Commission on the Arts, she works as a secondary school teacher in Columbus, Ohio.

VANESSA STAUFFER is a 2016 recipient of a Writer's Works in Progress grant from the Ontario Arts Council. She lives in Windsor, Ontario.

AMY STUBER's work has appeared in *The Antioch Review*, *New England Review*, *Ploughshares*, and elsewhere. Currently, she is working on a novel, of which "People's Parties" is a part. She lives in Lawrence, Kansas.

JESSICA LYNN SUCHON is a poet, essayist, and women's rights advocate. Her work has appeared or is forthcoming in *Cosmonauts Avenue*, *Hermeneutic Chaos*, *Radar Poetry*, and *Yemassee*, among others. She lives in Nashville, Tennessee.

IRA SUKRUNGRUANG is the author of three nonfiction books, most recently *Buddha's Dog & other Meditations* (U. of Tampa, 2018), as well as the short story collection *The Melting Season* (Burlesque, 2016) and the poetry collection *In Thailand It Is Night* (U. of Tampa, 2013). He is one of the founding editors of *Sweet: A Literary Confection* (sweetlit.com) and teaches in the MFA program at University of South Florida.

Mauritian poet **KHAL TORABULLY**, inventor of the postcolonial concept of "coolitude," is the author of more than a dozen poetry collections. For more information, see page 121.

JACINDA TOWNSEND is the author of *Saint Monkey* (Norton, 2014), and won the Janet Heidinger Kafka Prize and the James Fenimore Cooper Prize for historical fiction. A former Fulbright fellow in Côte d'Ivoire, she has recently finished a novel called *Kif*. She teaches in the writing program at UC Davis in California.

JESSICA TRAYNOR's debut collection *Liffey Swim* (Dedalus, 2014) was shortlisted for the Strong/Shine Award. A series of poems in response to Jonathan Swift's *A Modest Proposal* was commissioned by The Salvage Press in 2017. Her poems appear in *Acumen*, *Prelude*, *Rochford Street Review*, *Salamander*, and others. She lives in Dublin and is a freelance dramaturge at the Irish Theatre.

COREY VAN LANDINGHAM is the author of *Antidote*, winner of the 2012 OSU Press/The Journal Award in Poetry. Her work has appeared in *Best American Poetry 2014*, *Boston Review*, *Kenyon Review*, *The New Yorker*, and elsewhere. She's currently a book review editor for *The Kenyon Review* and lives in Ohio.

CHELSEA WAGENAAR is the author of *Mercy Spurs the Bone* (Anhinga, 2015), which won the 2013 Philip Levine Prize. Her poems and nonfiction appear or are forthcoming in *Grist*, *Poetry Northwest*, and *Southern Indiana Review*. She is a Lilly Fellow at Valparaiso University in Indiana.

CHRISTOPHER WARNER's poems have appeared in *Atlanta Review*, *Drunken Boat*, *Salamander*, *Spoon River Poetry Review*, and elsewhere. He works as a brakeman for Union Pacific Railroad and lives in central Illinois with his wife and three small boys.

JONATHAN WEINERT is the author of *In the Mode of Disappearance* (Nightboat, 2008), winner of the Nightboat Poetry Prize, and *Thirteen Small Apostrophes* (Back Pages, 2013), a chapbook. He is co-editor, with Kevin Prufer, of *Until Everything Is Continuous Again: American Poets on the Recent Work of W. S. Merwin* (WordFarm, 2014). He lives in Massachusetts.

MIKE WHITE is the author of two poetry collections: *Addendum to a Miracle* (Waywiser, 2017) and *How to Make a Bird with Two Hands* (Word Works, 2012). His work appears in *AGNI*, *The New Republic*, *Ploughshares*, *Poetry*, and elsewhere. Born and raised in Montreal, he holds citizenships in Canada and America and teaches at the University of Utah.

CHRISSY WILLIAMS has published a number of poetry pamphlets—most recently *This* (If a Leaf Falls, 2016), *Seven Poems* (HappenStance, 2014), and *Epigraphs* (if p then q, 2014)—and she edited the UK's first anthology of poetry comics: *Over the Line: An Introduction to Poetry Comics* (Sidekick, 2015). Her first full-length collection, *BEAR*, was published in 2017 by Bloodaxe. She lives in London.

Required Reading

(Issue 27)

(Each issue we ask that our contributors recommend up to three recent titles. What follows is the list generated by issue 27's contributors.)

Ghayath Almadhoun, *Adrenalin*, trans. Catherine Cobham (Caitlin Roach)

Lauren Arrington, *Revolutionary Lives: Constance and Casimir Markievicz* (Martin Dyar)

Zeina Hashem Beck, *Louder Than Hearts* (Farah Ali)

Peter Bd, *Milk & Henny* (Sam Riviere)

Adam Becker, *What Is Real? The Unfinished Quest for the Meaning of Quantum Physics* (John Koethe)

Brit Bennett, *The Mothers* (Jessica Lynn Suchon)

Claire Louise Bennett, *Pond* (Elaine Feeney)

Joshua Bennett, *The Sobbing School* (Christopher Kempf)

Tara Bergin, *The Tragic Death of Eleanor Marx* (Stephen Sexton)

Jamel Brinkley, *A Lucky Man* (Jacinda Townsend)

Lucie Brock-Broido, *Stay, Illusion* (Kathleen McGookey)

Ann Carson, *Float* (Jonathan Weinert)

Jennifer Chang, *Some Say the Lark* (Corey Van Landingham)

Teju Cole, *Blind Spot* (Kathryn Nuernberger)

Martha Collins, *Night Unto Night* (Christopher Kempf)

Sophie Collins, *Who Is Mary Sue?* (Chrissy Williams)

Stephen Corey, *Startled at the Big Sound: Essays Personal, Literary, and Cultural* (Nancy Naomi Carlson)

Claudia Cortese, *Wasp Queen* (Jessica Lynn Suchon)

Douglas Crase, *Astropastorals* (John Koethe)

Ailbhe Darcy, *Insistence* (Paul Perry)

Don DeLillo, *Zero K* (Benjamin S. Grossberg)

Stuart Dischell, *Children with Enemies* (Michael Pontacoloni)

Anthony Doerr, *All the Light We Cannot See* (Jacinda Townsend)

Camille Dungy, *Trophic Cascade* (T. R. Hummer)

Carolina Ebeid, *You Ask Me to Talk About the Interior* (Molly Spencer)

Claudia Emerson, *Claude Before Time and Space* (Benjamin S. Grossberg)

Mark Engler & Paul Engler, *This Is an Uprising: How Nonviolent Revolt Is Shaping the Twenty-First Century* (Jyotsna Sreenivasan)

Álvaro Enrigue, *Sudden Death*, trans. Natasha Wimmer (Jessica Traynor)

Tarfia Faizullah, *Registers of Illuminated Villages* (Francis Santana)

Sonia Farmer, *Infidelities* (Vahni Capildeo)

Elaine Feeney, *Rise* (Jessica Traynor)

Briony Fer, Francis Morris, Tiffany Bell, et al. *Agnes Martin* (L. S. Klatt)

Ariel Francisco, *All My Heroes Are Broke* (Juan Morales)

Aja Gabel, *The Ensemble* (Chelsea Wagenaar)

Roxane Gay, *Ayiti* (Amy Stuber)

Amy Gerstler, *Scattered at Sea* (Michael Homolka)

Galo Ghigliotto, *Valdivia*, trans. Daniel Borzutsky (Julia Leverone)

Adam Giannelli, *Tremulous Hinge* (David Keplinger)

Idris Goodwin & Kevin Coval, *Human Hightlight: An Ode to Dominique Wilkins* (Juan Morales)

Richard Gwyn, Ed., *The Pterodactyl's Wing: Welsh World Poetry* (Zoë Brigley)

Gabe Habash, *Stephen Florida* (Amy Stuber)

Maja Haderlap, *Angel of Oblivion*, trans. Tess Lewis (Nancy Naomi Carlson)

John Haines, *The Owl in the Mask of the Dreamer* (Christopher Warner)

Lauren Haldeman, *Instead of Dying* (Martin Dyar)

Mohsin Hamid, *Exit West* (Lorna Shaughnessy)

Diana Hamilton, *The Awful Truth* (Sam Riviere)

Jennifer Rane Hancock, *Between Hurricanes* (Juan Morales)

Shadab Zeest Hashmi, *Ghazal Cosmopolitan: The Culture and Craft of the Ghazal* (Hera Naguib)

Alan Hayes, Ed., *Washing Windows?: Irish Women Write Poetry* (Martin Dyar)

Oli Hazzard, *Blotter* (Chrissy Williams)

Lyn Hejinian, *The Unfollowing* (James Byrne)

Colin Herd, *Swamp Kiss* (Sam Riviere)

Marcelo Hernandez Castillo, *Cenzontle* (Jenny Boychuk)

Brenda Hillman, *Extra Hidden Life, among the Days* (Jonathan Weinert)

Homer, *The Odyssey*, trans. Emily Wilson (Vanessa Stauffer)

Garrett Hongo, *Coral Road* (T. R. Hummer)

Erica Hunt & Dawn Lundy Martin, Eds., *Letters to the Future: Black WOMEN/Radical WRITING* (Erika Jo Brown)

Ishion Hutchinson, *House of Lords and Commons* (Christopher Warner)

Amaan Hyder, *At Hajj* (Chrissy Williams)

Tayari Jones, *An American Marriage* (Emily Skaja)

Fady Joudah, *Footnotes in the Order of Disappearance* (David Keplinger)

Ilya Kaminsky, *Deaf Republic* (James Byrne)

Donika Kelly, *Bestiary* (Molly Spencer)

Amy Key, *Isn't Forever* (Stephen Sexton)

Porochista Khakpour, *Sick* (Emily J. Cousins)

Bill Knot, *I Am Flying Into Myself: Selected Poems* (Molly Spencer)

Jason Koo, *More Than Mere Light* (Arthur Russell)

Rachel Kushner, *The Mars Room* (Erika Jo Brown)

Lynn Kutsukake, *The Translation of Love* (Jyotsna Sreenivasan)

Lance Larsen, *What the Body Knows* (Mike White)

Nicholas Laughlin, *Fremd or Foe* (Vahni Capildeo)

Joseph Lease, *The Body Ghost* (Paul Perry)

Dell Lemon, *Single Woman* (Arthur Russell)

Dana Levin, *Banana Palace* (Paul Otremba)

James Longenbach, *Earthling* (Corey Marks)

Melissa Lozada-Oliva, *peluda* (Becka Mara McKay)

Sophie Macintosh, *The Water Cure* (Manuela Moser)

Rebecca Makkai, *The Great Believers* (Becka Mara McKay)

Carmen Maria Machado, *Her Body and Other Parties* (Jenny Boychuk, Emily J. Cousins, Jessica Lynn Suchon)

Hugh Martin, *In Country* (Christopher Kempf)

Imbolo Mbue, *Behold the Dreamers* (Jyotsna Sreenivasan)

Chris McCabe, *Dedalus* (James Byrne)

David McCullough, *The Wright Brothers* (Arthur Russell)

Gail McConnell, *Fourteen* (Vahni Capildeo)

Mike McCormack, *Solar Bones* (Elaine Feeney)

Karyna McGlynn, *Hothouse* (Vanessa Stauffer)

Adam Mcomber, *My House Gathers Desires* (Ira Sukrungruang)

Madeline Miller, *Circe* (Vanessa Stauffer)

David Mitchell, *The Thousand Autumns of Jacob de Zoet* (Benjamin S. Grossberg)

Rosalie Moffett, *June in Eden* (Corey Van Landingham)

Sinéad Morrissey, *On Balance* (Corey Marks)

Ottessa Moshfegh, *Eileen* (Farah Ali)

Hieu Minh Nguyen, *Not Here* (Paul Otremba)

Annemarie Ní Churreáin, *Bloodroot* (Paul Perry, Jessica Traynor)

Conor O'Callaghan, *Nothing on Earth* (Stephen Sexton)

Tommy Orange, *There There* (Amy Stuber)

José Orduña, *The Weight of Shadows: A Memoir of Immigration & Displacement*
   (Caitlin Roach)

Michael Parker, *Everything, Then and Since* (Michael Pontacoloni)

Sandeep Parmar, *Eidolon* (Vahni Capildeo)

Pascale Petit, *Mama Amazonica* (Lorna Shaughnessy)

John Pineda, *Let's No One Get Hurt* (Ira Sukrungruang)

Jacques Rancourt, *Novena* (Corey Van Landingham)

Shane Rhodes, *Dead White Men* (Erika Jo Brown)

Nina Riggs, *The Bright Hour: A Memoir of Living and Dying* (Kathleen McGookey)

David Roderick, *The Americans* (Michael Pontacoloni)

Sally Rooney, *Normal People* (Manuela Moser)

Mary Ruefle, *My Private Property* (Jonathan Weinert)

Selah Satterstrom, *Ideal Suggestions: Essays in Divinatory Poetics* (Kathryn Nuernberger)

Sam Sax, *Madness* (Francis Santana)

Julie Schumacher, *The Shakespeare Requirement* (Stuart Friebert)

David Schwartz, *The Last Man Who Knew Everything: The Life and Times of Enrico
   Fermi, Father of the Nuclear Age* (Stuart Friebert)

George Seferis, *Collected Poems*, trans. Keeley & Sherrard (Christopher Warner)

Diane Seuss, *Still Life with Two Dead Peacocks and a Girl* (Paul Otremba)

Raena Shirali, *Gilt* (Paige Quiñones)

Zadie Smith, *Feel Free* (Jacinda Townsend, Chelsea Wagenaar)

Lisa Russ Sparr, *Orexia* (Chelsea Wagenaar)

Megan Stielstra, *The Wrong Way to Save Your Life* (Emily Skaja)

Bianca Stone, *Möbius Strip Club of Grief* (Paige Quiñones)

Kelly Sundberg, *Goodbye, Sweet Girl* (Julia Leverone)

Mary Szybist, *Incarnadine* (Lorna Shaughnessy)

Abigail Thomas, *Safekeeping: Some True Stories from a Life* (Ira Sukrungruang)

Angie Thomas, *The Hate U Give* (Emily Skaja)

Elizabeth Thomas, *The Hidden Life of Dogs* (Stuart Friebert)

Pimone Triplett, *Supply Chain* (Corey Marks)

Sarah Viren, *MINE* (Becka Mara McKay)

Jesmyn Ward, *Sing, Unburied, Sing* (Jenny Boychuk)

Sarah Waters, *Fingersmith* (Zoë Brigley)

Lisa Wells, *The Fix* (Caitlin Roach)

Shawn Wen, *A Twenty Minute Silence Followed by Applause* (Kathryn Nuernberger)

Charlotte Williams, *Sugar and Slate* (Zoë Brigley)

Joy Williams, *Ninety-Nine Stories of God* (David Keplinger)

Joy Williams, *The Visiting Privilege* (L. S. Klatt)

C. Dale Young, *The Affliction* (Francis Santana)

Javier Zamora, *Unaccompanied* (Emily J. Cousins, Julia Leverone)

Samantha Zighelboim, *The Fat Sonnets* (Elaine Feeney)

The Copper Nickel Editors' Prizes

(est. 2015)

(Two $500 prizes awarded to the most exciting work published in each issue,
as determined by a vote of the *Copper Nickel* staff)

Past Winners

spring 2018 (issue 26)

Cindy Tran, poetry; Gianni Skaragas, prose

fall 2017 (issue 25)

Sarah Carson, poetry; Meagan Ciesla, prose

spring 2017 (issue 24)

Ashley Keyser, poetry; Robert Long Foreman, prose

fall 2016 (issue 23)

Tim Carter, poetry; Evelyn Somers, prose

spring 2016 (issue 22)

Bernard Farai Matambo, poetry; Sequoia Nagamatsu, prose

fall 2015 (issue 21)

Jonathan Weinert, poetry; Tyler Mills, prose

spring 2015 (issue 20)

Michelle Oakes, poetry; Donovan Ortega, prose

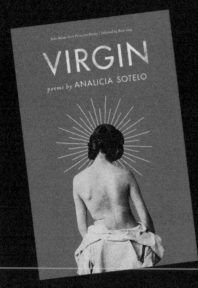

COPPERNICKEL

subscription rates

For regular folks:

one year (two issues)—$20
two years (four issues)—$35
three years (six issues)—$45
five years (ten issues)—$60

For student folks:

one year (two issues)—$15
two years (four issues)—$23
three years (six issues)—$32
five years (ten issues)—$50

For more information, visit: www.copper-nickel.org.

To go directly to subscriptions
visit: www.regonline.com/coppernickelsubscriptions.

To order back issues, call 303-315-7358
or email wayne.miller@ucdenver.edu